DON'T STOP THE ROLLER COASTER

DON'T STOP THE ROLLER COASTER

BUSINESS AND LIFE LESSONS

BY TOM DePETRILLO

BRIGANTINE MEDIA

Don't Stop the Roller Coaster

Copyright © 2014 by Tom DePetrillo

All rights reserved. No part of this book may be reproduced or utilized in any way or by any means, electronic or mechanical, including photocopying, recording, or any information storage or retrieval system without permission in writing from the publisher.

Cover and Book Design by Jacob L. Grant

ISBN 978-1-9384063-0-0

Brigantine Media
211 North Avenue
St. Johnsbury, Vermont 05819
Phone: 802-751-8802
Email: neil@brigantinemedia.com
Website: www.brigantinemedia.com

DEDICATION

To my wife,
Carol

ACKNOWLEDGMENTS

Thank you to my family and friends who were there at
every step to help and encourage me in this project.
Thanks also to Brigantine Media
for making the book happen.

TABLE OF CONTENTS

Introduction..**1**

PART ONE – LIFE ON THE ROLLER COASTER
Family...**7**
Education...**15**
Early Career...**21**
Hard Lessons...**29**
Deals..**41**

PART TWO – WHAT I LEARNED ON THE ROLLER COASTER
Wall Street..**61**
Government..**77**
Health Care...**99**
Politics...**109**

Afterword..**125**

INTRODUCTION

Far better it is to dare mighty things, to win glorious triumphs even though checkered by failure, than to take rank with those poor spirits who neither enjoy nor suffer much, because they live in the gray twilight that knows neither victory or defeat.

THEODORE ROOSEVELT
(26th US president, 1858-1919)

My life in business has been a fascinating roller coaster ride, and I've enjoyed all its twists and turns. I wrote this book to help other people profit from my insights and avoid my mistakes.

I firmly believe that a person's destiny is not controlled by where he or she was born, the wealth of his or her family, or the number of diplomas he or she hangs on the wall. To achieve real and lasting success, a person needs a lifelong desire to learn and a burning compulsion to always reach higher.

I've achieved professional and personal success I could not imagine when I was growing up in the projects in Providence, Rhode Island. I hope that in this book, I can describe what went right for me and where I took a wrong turn. I'm hoping this information will help other people achieve their goals.

I have been the recipient of a lot of help throughout my life. People have taken a chance on me. Government programs offered assistance to me. I was even helped to get a fresh start when I hit rock bottom early in my career.

Many people think the government should just get out of the way and let the "invisible hand" of the market do its magic. But if we eliminate all government assistance, we will be consigning some people to failure who might otherwise prosper. I am not a subscriber to the conservative school of governing, which I think assumes that half the population just wants a handout.

Being a successful businessperson does not necessarily translate into being a successful politician. Take the most recent Republican presidential candidate, Mitt Romney, who had a successful business career commanding people to do exactly what he wanted.

But you can't run the government like a business. A business wouldn't distribute food stamps. Business qualities such as leadership and confidence translate into politics, but politics is not a moneymaking enterprise. You have to serve the poor as well as the rich. A businessman just doesn't think that way. I know because I am a businessman, not a politician. But I contribute to politicians who I think can make a difference in people's lives and who support programs and policies I agree with.

I think government and private enterprise can work hand-in-hand to help build our country and serve the public interest. I believe our country will be better off if people adopt these five ideas that my experience on the roller coaster have taught me:

1. Give people a helping hand when they need it the most.
2. Just because you fail at some point in your life does not make you a failure. You may need to make a fresh start.
3. Wall Street is an insiders' game and not for most small investors.
4. Health care is a right, not a privilege. Big business shouldn't drive health care policy.
5. Public education can work, but not if we allow education to become a for-profit industry. Put that money into education programs that can really help people.

I believe that with compassion and assistance, more people can be successful. Our current political debate is often between tone-deaf wealthy people and some liberals who do not understand the needs of the financial sector. Let's tone down the rhetoric and have a more productive dialogue about how we can help more people manage the ups and downs in their own journey through life. I hope my story can be an example and an inspiration to people, showing them that with drive and determination, they can ride the roller coaster to the top.

PART ONE

Life on the Roller Coaster

Family

*The love of family and the admiration of friends
is much more important than wealth and privilege.*
CHARLES KURALT
(American journalist, 1934-1997)

I start and end this book with my family, the main source of strength and inspiration for my success.

I credit much of what I have accomplished to my upbringing. Growing up, there were eleven children in my family, and our roller coaster economic condition helped prepare me for life's up and downs. Most of the time we were at the low end of the economic scale, but there was plenty of love and caring to nurture all of us. Growing up without much money gave me a lot of empathy for people in difficult circumstances. I know for a fact that being poor or being a new immigrant does not have to keep you from fulfilling your ambitions.

My mother was named Fatima because her uncle was in Portugal when the Apparition of Fatima occurred. She was put in an orphanage at the age of five. My dad's name was Francisco, but everyone called him Frank.

My father's family was one of the first Italian families to settle in Providence, Rhode Island. My grandfather on my father's side was a jewelry maker, barber, and had other odd jobs. He loved to fix things. My father's mother was a midwife.

When my mother was fifteen, she was a foster child and took care of another family's younger children. One day, my dad was playing the violin at a christening in a neighbor's yard. My mom watched from the porch and my father serenaded her. A social worker played matchmaker and told my mother, "This is a good guy from a good family. You should get together." My parents got married and almost immediately started having kids—and they didn't stop until there were eleven of us.

My father was a jack-of-all-trades. Besides working in the shipyard, playing the violin, and making jewelry, he was also an inventor. He had only a fourth grade education, but enough intellect to obtain a United States patent on the complex mathematical formula needed to mechanically reproduce the logarithmic spiral. It was called the "Spiral of DePetrillo."

A logarithmic spiral, also known as an equiangular spiral or growth spiral, is a special kind of spiral curve that only appears in nature. It was first described by Descartes and later extensively investigated by Jacob Bernoulli, who called it *spira mirabilis*, "the marvelous spiral."

After perfecting his invention, my father went to a patent attorney to protect his intellectual property. His invention was the first mechanical device to reproduce the spiral form found in nature. The patent clearly stated that whenever this spiral was used in jewelry or manufacturing, it would be called the "Spiral of DePetrillo."

His machine, a collection of gears and odd-shaped parts, turned out an endless stream of spirals in wire form that could be used in everything from jewelry to screen doors. In the early 1950s, he was hired to produce hundreds of thousands of spirals for a company that produced ornamental carafes.

My oldest brother worked with my father producing the spirals. Unfortunately, after six months, the company stole my dad's invention and moved the production to Florida. My father sued, but he did not have the capital to pursue a large, well-funded company.

The machine my father invented ended up in the cellar, where it stayed for many years. This episode left my dad feeling swindled and demoralized. I was just a kid, but what happened to my dad made a big impression on me. I learned it was not enough just to be smart. To succeed in the world you had to have the *right* kind of smarts. My father had no business experience and paid a heavy price.

I was determined not to let anyone take advantage of me. I also learned at an early age that you must move on quickly after adversity. You can't let one stroke of bad luck ruin your life.

Our family's fortunes ebbed and flowed. As the number of children in our family increased, my parents found it hard to afford shoes or eyeglasses or many things we needed.

>
> I was determined not to let anyone take advantage of me. I also learned at an early age that you must move on quickly after adversity. You can't let one stroke of bad luck ruin your life.

We had three bedrooms in our home: my parents' room, the girls' room, and the boys' room. Since there were seven boys, we learned about sharing very early. I remember plenty of happy times, but often, money was short and my father had trouble supporting such a large family. One by one the older brothers had to leave school and get jobs to support the family. I looked for a way to get out of the house and on my own as quickly as I could. I loved my family, but I wanted to get on with my life.

I went to work full time at age sixteen. None of the older boys in the family finished high school. It was a blow to the family when my brother Frank quit school, because he was at the top of his class. When he quit, his teacher came to our house to try to convince my parents to let him stay in school.

During our rough financial times, our family was the beneficiary of some charity—mostly free summer camps and Christmas gifts. I spent many of my summers at camps at no cost to my family. When I was ten years old, I went to a camp in Narragansett,

Rhode Island. Campers were selected by the Providence police, who chose kids who stayed out of trouble. When you arrived at camp, you handed over any money you brought to the camp, and it was held in a credit account at the canteen for you. At the end of the day, the canteen was opened and campers could use their money to buy candy and other treats.

> I've often found that people with big incomes don't understand the value of a few dollars to someone who has no money. But I do. I learned that lesson very early on.

I had no money when I came to camp that year. When the mother of a friend of mine from the projects found out I had nothing to put in the canteen, she gave me fifty cents for my canteen account. This money made all the difference in the world to me. Fifty cents could pay for ten separate items! My favorites were Jujyfruits and cupcakes, and I spread the fifty cents out over the six nights I spent there. It was my first opportunity to learn how to manage money.

But I learned an even more important lesson than money management from that fifty cents. That money allowed me to feel just like all the other campers when we lined up every night at the canteen. Her small gift was a very big deal to me.

I've often found that people with big incomes don't understand the value of a few dollars to someone who has no money. But I do. I learned that lesson very early on.

We live in the wealthiest country on earth, and fortune has smiled on many of us. But money has become something of a false idol in America for many people.

What counts is not your bank account, or your earnings from playing the stock market, or the riches that can be made on Wall Street or in real estate. What counts are greater principles such as economic justice on the societal level and self-fulfillment on an individual level. Having money is nice, but it can't buy happiness, love, or true friendship. Having money is nice, but it is a blessing only if you use share some of it to help your community and those less fortunate than you.

The most important qualities in life are found within yourself. You have to learn what your talents are as well as your limitations. My family gave me the self-confidence and moral support to face the world, no matter what I encountered. But it also gave me the insight to recognize that those who are fortunate can, with a little generosity, make a big difference in the lives of others.

I married for the first time when I was twenty, and my wife was only eighteen. After a few years, I knew that the marriage wasn't going to work out. But we have three wonderful children from that union, and it taught me some insight about what makes a strong marriage.

I met my wife, Carol, in 1980, a few years after the breakup of my first marriage. I call her my "uptown girl" — she already had her Master's in education and was in law school in Boston at the time. She has had a very successful legal career, first as a public defender and then a prosecutor for the state of Rhode Island, and later, in her own practice. Thirty-three years later, we are still as much in love as the day we married. Carol is a major reason why I could concentrate on my career, knowing I always had her support. I have been so lucky throughout my life to have the emotional backing of family. I know from my own experience the importance of a loving family to success in life.

Education

It is a thousand times better to have common sense without education than to have education without common sense.

ROBERT GREEN INGERSOLL
(American political leader and orator, 1833-1899)

I consider myself well educated.

But I didn't get my education through the normal route. I never fit the mold. I followed a path that took me to work *before* education, not the other way around. Some people, out of necessity or preference, start work early. I was one of those types, anxious to help my family financially and get out on my own.

My case is an example of how false starts can sometimes lead to good results. I wanted to learn, but I rebelled so much against the standard educational structure I almost lost any chance to get a good education.

When I first went to school, I put up such a fuss that the school sent me home. I started again the next year, so my younger brother Larry and I were in the same grade.

My teacher, Mrs. Clifford, made me sit in the wastebasket because I was such a troublemaker. It wasn't my teachers' fault that I had such a hard time. If they were trying to teach me about American history, I wanted to read science fiction. If I was growing up today, I might be classified as ADHD, but in those days, I was just annoying.

I was always doing something different than the rest of kids. I wasn't a follower. In junior high school, my science teacher knew I was interested in radios and electronics, and he let me skip some classes to work on my science fair project. I ended up skipping English class a lot.

Because my family moved frequently, I attended six schools by the ninth grade. The principal of the last school I attended wanted to hold me back to take extra courses to get ready for high school, but I was older than the other students in my grade already. I left school when I was fifteen and a half. I worked in a relative's pizza restaurant until I turned sixteen, and then I got a job in a jewelry factory making one dollar an hour.

Although I wasn't a success in school, I always liked to learn. I devoured the *Encyclopedia Britannica* at home. My parents paid one dollar a week for the *Britannica* on credit, and it provided me with knowledge on a wide variety of subjects. I loved to read science magazines, too, and was a ham radio operator. At fifteen years old, I received a commercial license to operate a radio station.

My first educational break came from an unexpected place — the army. With seven boys in our family, we almost had our own recruiting officer. Sergeant Russo would come by once a week, have coffee with my parents, and see which son he could recruit next.

Eventually, five of us served in the military.

I was not an easy recruit. I insisted the only reason that I would join was to further my education. Specifically, I wanted a school that would prepare me for the space age.

The army school I wanted required me to take the GED test to get in, since I never attended high school. I passed the test with flying colors. My school also required a top secret clearance, which I also received.

I went through basic training in two months. From there I was sent to Red Stone Arsenal in Alabama to learn about electronics and missiles, which, at the time, had simple electronics but complicated mechanical components.

Our class was invited to see the first firing of the Jupiter missile engines that were early versions of the rockets eventually developed to send the first astronauts to the moon. I met Wernher von Braun, father of rocket science (and former Nazi) who was running our missile program. I learned what was considered advanced electronics at the time, before the advent of solid-state electronics.

When my one year of technical training was finished, the army sent me to Germany to work on missile systems. I also enrolled in the University of Maryland through extension courses provided for military personnel. I completed two years of college in that program.

In Germany, we worked in a factory with over two hundred German employees and fifty Americans.

Our job was to work on an improved V2 missile called the Corporal Missile.

After three years in the military, I decided to try civilian life again. My high level training and a top secret security clearance qualified me to land a job working as an outside contractor to General Electric. I spent the next four years working on highly classified government projects such as the spy-in-the-sky program.

My last engineering job was at the technology company Raytheon. I was 25 years old and if I had stayed at Raytheon, I could have been set financially for life.

But I had a restless personality. I didn't want to work for Raytheon for the rest of my life. I was interested in working in finance. I applied to a number of financial firms, and after some rejections, I eventually got hired at Kidder, Peabody.

That couldn't happen today. Now, a financial firm wants to hire trained MBA graduates at the top of the class. They don't want to spend tens of thousands of dollars training someone like me who didn't know anything about business.

But in 1965, Kidder, Peabody took a chance on me. I spent a year in training. During the last three months of training, I was with Kidder, Peabody's biggest producer in Boston.

Looking back on my education, there were a number of factors that led to my success:

- I wasn't willing to do what everybody else did.

- I had a strong internal desire to learn.
- I concentrated on subjects that really interested me.
- The military and several companies provided me with great training.
- I received training in areas that made a difference in my life.

I think educational accomplishment is not as much the result of the school you went to, but how much you have learned since you were in school.

No one questions the value of a college education, but when I see people my age wearing tee shirts from their alma mater, I wonder: Is this because of the kinship they still feel for their schools or because of the knowledge they learned while there? Knowledge is what really counts. A college degree will get your foot in the door, but it's what you do once inside that determines where you will go in business or in life.

> What counts is not the diploma you hang on your wall or the tee shirt you wear to the football game, but the knowledge you gain through studying and how you use it to further your career and life.

My formal education ended at ninth grade, but the value of learning was a principle I embraced when I was growing up with parents who challenged us to think and learn. My parents taught me the lifelong values of persistence and hard work.

In my businesses, I have employed countless college graduates. But I judge my employees by what they do now, not where they went to school then, or what grade level they completed. The record shows my formal education ended at ninth grade, but in business matters, I would certainly say that I have the equivalent of a PhD. What counts is not the diploma you hang on your wall or the tee shirt you wear to the football game, but the knowledge you gain through studying and how you use it to further your career and life.

Early Career

*There are no secrets to success.
It is the result of preparation, hard work,
and learning from failure.*
COLIN POWELL
(US four-star general and 65th Secretary of State, b. 1937)

Although I had been trained as an engineer to work on missile systems, I decided fairly early in my working career that I wanted something different. My first job after leaving the military was with a contractor for General Electric. GE had the Spy in the Sky program—the first satellite that had cameras and revolved around the earth. My contract was for $25,000 for one year, the equivalent of over $150,000 today. Not bad for a high school dropout!

From General Electric in Syracuse I went to General Electric in Radnor, Pennsylvania; Burroughs Corp. in West Chester, Pennsylvania; Westinghouse in Baltimore; then Raytheon in Norwood, Massachusetts.

I bought thirteen acres of land in Greenville, Rhode Island and built a house for my family and developed housing lots for sale. I also bought a franchise from an electronics chain called Lafayette Radio Electronics

Corporation and opened up a retail store in Providence with two of my brothers. I continued to work at Raytheon while I worked at the store on nights and weekends. This was at the peak of the CB radio craze. The store did well for two years and then sales started to slow down. We closed the store when the CB fad ended.

These outside projects made me realize that I was not suited to a desk job as an engineer. I wanted to work in sales, but I wanted to sell intangible products, not radios and electronics equipment.

I thought about what I could sell that did not require an investment in inventory. Real estate required too much capital. I didn't like the idea of being an insurance salesman. I decided to try the securities industry, and I made that decision on a leap of faith. No one in my family had ever owned a security and I really did not understand the financial markets. I bought a few books to learn the basics and looked into entering a training program offered by a major financial firm.

I arranged twelve interviews with financial firms, and no one offered me a job. After a lot of rejections, I interviewed with Paine Webber. The interviewer said the same thing I had heard over and over: I had a technical background, no college degree, no financial background, and I was too high a risk for a year-long training program. He could not understand why I would give up my job paying $25,000 a year for a starting salary of $5,000. But he offered to send me to his friend Robert Goldhammer at Kidder, Peabody.

Goldhammer told me to come over that day. When

I arrived at his office, he said he had heard that I was willing to give up a high-paying job to start as a trainee. But did I *really* know what being a stockbroker was?

I said yes, it was a selling job.

He said, "You're hired! No one around here wants to admit they are salespeople. They all want to be investment bankers or research analysts. I need more salespeople."

I was thrilled. I knew I had the drive, energy, and enthusiasm to make it in the financial world.

I spent the next year commuting between Boston and New York in a fabulous training program. Part of the training was learning how to sell. The top salesmen at Kidder, Peabody would tell stories about how they became successful. I realized quickly that I had the ability to sell. I enjoyed talking to people and I was quick to pick up on selling techniques.

I started selling securities in early 1966 when the Dow Jones was under 1,000. After a year of training, which was a helpful introduction to the business, I was assigned to the retail division of the Providence office, where I was required to make a certain number of cold calls per day and per month. I knew almost no one with money, so cold calling was my only option to drum up some business.

Kidder, Peabody had a formula for building a client list: "Make one hundred cold phone calls. From those one hundred calls, you'll develop ten leads. Eventually, you'll make a sale."

But I figured out two things. One, I didn't want

to make one hundred cold calls. I wanted to go after wealthy people and business owners who I knew would have some money to invest. And two, I realized after a few years that I didn't want to be a salesman. The big money was in investment banking. I wanted to swim with the big fish.

My boss, Dana Djerf, taught me a little trick. He told me to check the business pages of the newspaper, where companies listed business people who had recently been promoted. Typical listings would say that Joe Smith has just been named vice president at Acme Enterprises, Jill Miller is now head of advertising at Widget Inc., etc. I called these recently promoted people, who usually had received a raise with their promotion, and congratulated them. I asked if I might call on them. I never tried to make a sale on the phone, and not even on that first visit. I left every visit with a promise to get back in touch when I found an idea that person might want.

I came across the name of Stephen Hassenfeld in the paper. He had just been promoted to vice president of marketing at Hasbro, which was, and still is, headquartered in Pawtucket, Rhode Island.

The people in the office laughed at me when I mentioned his name. Stephen Hassenfeld? He was just 25 years old. His family did own a company but it was just a toy company. They'd had a hit with G.I. Joe, but how long could that last? Toys hardly ranked with the big industrials or the emerging technology companies.

Little did my fellow brokers know Hasbro was

destined for great business success. In 2011, Hasbro had record sales of $4.9 billion, placing it just outside the Fortune 500. With brilliant marketing and masterful development of core brands such as G.I. Joe, Monopoly, and Playskool, along with new launches and successful forays into movies such as the *Transformers* franchise, it has long reigned as one of America's most profitable and innovative companies. It is also one of America's top philanthropic firms, through the Hassenfeld Family Initiatives, run now by Alan Hassenfeld, who succeeded his older brother Stephen as CEO and chairman of the company.

But the early years, there was little indication of Hasbro's future success. Despite the derisive talk around my Kidder, Peabody office, I called Stephen, and he invited me to visit with him. As I was leaving, I asked Stephen if he would be interested in my calling him if I ever found a suitable investment. He agreed.

I let two weeks pass, then called to see if he was interested in shares of new stock for twelve dollars a share. He told me to put fifty shares, a net investment of $600, into the Hassenfeld Foundation. That stock opened at $110 a share, netting the foundation a profit of almost $5,000, virtually overnight. From that day on, I was close to Stephen and to his family and their foundations. We did several deals and were involved in charity work together.

After about six months at Kidder, Peabody, I told Djerf that I wanted to switch to a commission-based salary. I had been drawing $500 a month straight pay.

> The smaller your clients are, the more of your time they want. The amount of time I spent on a typical one hundred-share order was about the same amount of time I spent on a one thousand-share order. In effect, I was being paid ten times more per hour to work on one thousand-share orders.

Under company rules, an employee who switched to commission could never go back to draw. It was sink or swim.

"You're crazy," Dana said. No one had ever switched that fast.

But I was confident in my ability to sell a lot of shares and earn significant commissions. Even at this stage of my career, I had learned an important lesson about making money as a stockbroker. If I received an order for one hundred shares, a typical order for me, I made a $45 commission. But a broker who had been at Kidder, Peabody for ten years and sold a one thousand-share lot made a $450 commission. I thought to myself, "Why can't I sell one thousand-share lots?" So I got rid of all of my one hundred-share commission business, and I only worked on orders of one thousand shares more. I cut my order book by two-thirds in one year. It was very tough to make a decision to give up so much business. But in taking those smaller share orders, I wasn't valuing my time enough.

The smaller your clients are, the more of your time they want. The amount of time I spent on a typical one hundred-share order was about the same amount of time I spent on a one thousand-share order. In effect, I was being paid ten times more per hour to work on one thousand-share orders.

At the end of two years, I was making $50,000 in commissions; after three years, over $100,000 a year in commissions. I had the State of Rhode Island's Treasurers' office doing business with me. Working with the larger clients was definitely a strong factor in my success as a stockbroker.

In 1968, the Hassenfeld family, led by Stephen, who was turning out to be a major force at Hasbro, decided to take the company public. I brought the deal to my manager and he sent it to our headquarters in New York. At the time, Hasbro's annual sales were just under $50 million. Kidder, Peabody turned it down, saying that the deal was too small and in an unattractive industry. I referred Hasbro to a smaller local firm to do the underwriting. Several months after the company went public, the stock was trading a few points lower than the original offering price. Steven called me to ask if there was anything I could do to support the price. I went to a mutual fund manager in Boston and made a deal. We found buyers for 200,000 shares of stock, which caused the stock price to increase from eight dollars to twelve dollars a share.

When it came time to allocate the commission from the trading in the stock, every penny went to the Boston Kidder, Peabody office, and none to me. I complained, but was told, that's the rule — retail brokers like me were not allowed to handle institutional transactions.

So I left Kidder, Peabody. There were three other companies for whom I was raising money that were interested in going public, but I would have had to give up being a stockbroker to work on Kidder, Peabody's institutional side.

Instead, I started my own investment firm, Advance Technology Development Corporation (AVTEK), which combined my long expertise in electronics with the investment skills I learned at Kidder, Peabody. I was off and running.

Because of the connections I had made with wealthy investors, I was able to raise two million dollars to start my company. My first investors were the Hassenfelds. I was only 28 years old at the time, and I was full of confidence, even though we started our company with no particular business in mind. We were on the lookout to buy fundamentally sound businesses that needed additional capital and expertise to progress.

We created a mini-conglomerate by diversifying our investments. Our main businesses were jewelry, motor homes, mobile homes, and snowmobiles. After making some opportune purchases, we were able to take our company public at six dollars a share. We had quickly achieved success. Maybe too quickly.

Hard Lessons

Life deals you a lot of lessons.
Some people learn from it, some people don't.
BRETT FAVRE
(Retired football quarterback, b. 1969)

AVTEK

At our height, AVTEK had two thousand employees, but our company didn't have a strong internal infrastructure. We expanded too fast, and we did not have enough quality employees in top positions. We weren't sufficiently prepared for a downturn in business. We weren't prepared for a substantial change in economic conditions.

In 1973, oil spiked due to an unexpected oil embargo by OPEC following the United States support of Israel during the 1973 Yom Kippur war. The sales of recreational vehicles and mobile homes went down overnight because of the huge jump in the price of oil. At the time, $35 million of our $50 million annual revenues came from sales of recreational vehicles and mobile homes. Our entire business was at risk.

Before the downturn in sales, we had acquired the

>
> If you owe the banks a lot of money, you actually have a lot of leverage. Look at Donald Trump. He owed the banks so much money they couldn't afford to let him go under!

Northeast distributor of snowmobile manufacturer Arctic Cat. When he found we were running into some financial problem, the previous owner of Arctic Cat became interested in buying AVTEK. I was in favor of the sale because I didn't have the experience to deal with our bankers in this time of financial crisis.

I presented the offer to buy our company to my directors and key employees. They were all against the deal. Because of their reluctance to sell, I decided to stay the course. I knew we were going through difficult times, but I didn't think we were going to go under.

After missing this opportunity to sell, our business continued to go downhill. After oil prices shot up, there was a credit crunch. I had grown the company too fast, and I wasn't expert enough to save the company. I needed a high-quality operational staff that might have been able to survive a financial crisis, but we didn't have sufficient expertise.

I told our bankers, "For the good of the company, I have to leave."

Today, I wouldn't have let the banks run all over

me. I would have gone to the banks in a totally different way. If you owe the banks a lot of money, you actually have a lot of leverage. Look at Donald Trump. He owed the banks so much money they couldn't afford to let him go under!

I had personally signed a note at one bank for two million dollars, but I didn't think that was at risk, even after I gave up operational control, because our company had plenty of assets. But within a year, the company had lost so much money, the bank came back to me and demanded that I pay my two million dollar guarantee.

My lawyer told me to offer the bank $100,000, and if the bank wanted more, I should file for bankrupcy. I made that offer of $100,000 to the bank, but they didn't accept it.

So I went bankrupt. It was hard at first. My house was gone. My car was gone. My life changed.

But leaving the company I started wasn't difficult. The burden of carrying the weight of the company and trying to make everything right was more than a full-time job. Once I resigned, someone else had to worry about it.

I never lost confidence in my own abilities during this period of time. I knew I could make money. I had suffered a major setback, but deep down, I knew I could come back. I found consulting jobs almost immediately and continued to support my wife and three children. If I hadn't filed for bankruptcy, the bank would have owned me for the rest of my life. Bankruptcy wiped out my debt. The bank made a couple hundred thousand

> Bankruptcy is a useful tool when used under the right circumstances. It can protect you from your creditors. It gives you an opportunity to start over when you need it the most.

dollars on my assets and I was able to walk away.

Bankruptcy is a useful tool when used under the right circumstances. It can protect you from your creditors. It gives you an opportunity to start over when you need it the most.

Going bankrupt also protected me from my bankers. I learned that that you can't count on bankers to look after your interests. For many bankers, it's strictly business. If you're behind on the mortgage and a bank can make money on your house, many banks will foreclose on you in a second. No matter what they tell you, most managers at banks are more concerned about their jobs than they are about you.

But don't misunderstand me. Bankers can be extremely important in reaching your business goals. I have had bankers make very helpful investments in my business and me. But the bottom line is that banks will not always be helpful when you are struggling financially.

Even though my company collapsed, my five years running AVTEK taught me some important lessons:

1. Don't over-leverage yourself. I borrowed too heavily, and if I had been more conservatively capitalized, I might have been able to survive some tough circumstances.

2. Do not put all your trust in the banks. They may be happy to lend to you, but they must also protect their jobs and their stockholders. They will not be your saviors if your business is in deep trouble, unless it is in their financial benefit to do so.

3. The most important part of running a business, besides having a good business plan, is to have the right people. I want my employees to know more than I do in their areas of expertise so that they can keep the company operating profitably.

I expected a lot from my AVTEK employees and they couldn't deliver. My bankruptcy was as much a people failure as it was a financial failure. Today, I am much more cautious about putting my faith into untested employees and managers.

One of the lessons my adventure with AVTEK taught me is that if you put all your eggs in one basket (and for me at that point in my life my one basket was

AVTEK), you limit your opportunity to overcome tough times. Diversifying your investments helps you overcome adversity.

These days, I am often asked for financial advice. I'm very happy to help other people learn from my experience and my mistakes. One of the more common questions I am asked is what should someone do to get out of a fiscal mess.

> A person's true strengths and weaknesses come out in a crisis.

As a rule of thumb, the more choices available, the better the potential outcome. Think of the venture capitalist in the enviable position of being able to select one of the hundred deals they are offered. Or the person who can choose from two job offers, not just one. When everything seems to come together and you are coasting, your opportunities seem to be greatest.

But when things are difficult, when you are in a fiscal mess, you often work harder with fewer options. When you need something to happen, when you need that lucky break, it never seems to materialize.

Take the example of someone who has lost his job, is behind on the bills and the mortgage, and is getting by on credit cards and loans. In this difficult economy, there are many people in this type of situation. Most people react to such circumstances by trying to hang on, hoping things will get better in a few months and doing their best to stem the bleeding in the meantime. It's a depressing plight for anyone.

My advice: Go to zero. Seek bankruptcy if you have to. Clean the slate and start fresh. This advice is not for someone who has had a minor setback. But for a severe financial setback (such as an unexpected medical hardship or a business failure), bankruptcy can make sense. Why continue for months down a long depressing road, when the outcome in the end will be the same: bankruptcy and possible foreclosure?

> Cutting losses makes sense both financially and psychologically. Don't get embittered and depressed about a continuing losing proposition. Go to zero. Start over.

This solution is *only* to be used in a real economic emergency, like the one caused by the bursting of the real estate bubble in 2007-2008. You can't use this reset button too often. But most people are too optimistic. I know that because I'm an optimistic person and that sometimes works against me. If you don't have to go bankrupt, don't go bankrupt. If you can afford the payments on your house or your business, hang on to it. But if you are drowning because you can't afford your obligations, start over.

This advice applies both to individuals and to business owners. Take the example of someone who mortgages his house to open a restaurant. In the first year, he makes a few dollars but the second year brings losses, and the third year brings even bigger losses that force him to close the business. He would have been better off to get out earlier in the second year.

Cutting losses makes sense both financially and psychologically. Don't get embittered and depressed about a continuing losing proposition. Go to zero. Start over.

If there is a caveat, it's that my advice is intended primarily for younger people, who have more time ahead of them to recover and forge ahead. Older people should be more cautious and hopefully are not faced with overwhelming financial problems. But as people work longer, even older people may benefit from a fresh start.

My biggest business failure did not short-circuit my financial or personal life, because I took the important step of putting my failure behind me. The lessons I learned in restarting helped me survive financially the rest of my life.

PROVIDENCE SECURITIES

In the fall of 1987, my company, Providence Securities, was doing well. A boutique underwriting and retail firm, we employed three hundred people, mostly in Rhode Island, Florida, and New York. I was the majority stockholder, and some of our management and top salespeople owned the balance of the company's stock. As a relatively small firm by Wall Street standards, we did not handle our own back office paperwork, but instead, hired a larger firm to do the accounting for our customers' trades.

On Monday, October 19, 1987, the markets around the world crashed in what became known as "Black Monday." The Dow Jones was at 2,600 at the start of the day and ended at 2,100, a twenty percent drop, equivalent to a 3,000-point drop in the Dow today. There was absolute panic in the markets. Hundreds of billions of dollars were lost in market value and the entire financial sector of our economy was affected.

When we received our daily accounts the next morning, our working capital had dropped by two million dollars and the firm's net capital reserves were below what was required by the regulators. We didn't have enough capital to continue business normally. I was shocked. I assumed some of our customers had suffered major losses and would not or could not pay for their purchases, but the amount of our capital hit was way beyond what I expected. Where did the two million dollar loss come from?

It turned out a broker in one of our Florida offices had been trading options in a way that made it look like he had cash in his personal account. This was before the computerization of Wall Street, and when you made an option sale, it showed up as cash in your account and you had seven days to deliver the underlying stock. If you sold before the certificate was due, you received the profit or loss in your account.

The broker was trading illegally without authorization. It was the responsibility of our clearing firm to be aware of this kind of trading and prevent it. The broker was trading highly speculative options, and the big drop in the market caused his scheme to unravel. The broker's criminal activity resulted in large losses, costing us $1.5 million of the $2 million deficit. If our loss from "Black Monday" had been what I had anticipated, about $500,000, we could have dealt with the loss and we would not have violated the exchanges' capital requirements.

This drop in our capital resulted in two problems: insufficient working capital and a potential regulatory problem. The National Association of Securities Dealers (NASD) did oversight of smaller firms, and initially I was not worried, because I knew that most Wall Street firms had the same sort of capital problems since the crash.

I sold every stock and bond I owned and collateralized my real estate and personal assets with a bank to cover the losses. I am proud of the fact that not one of our customers lost a dollar and the firm never lost one day of business.

Some of my partners were not as supportive of our firm. My top salesperson went into a depression and left the firm to go with another brokerage firm that offered him a signing bonus. Some of the other employees were very loyal, but they did not have the capital or experience to save our firm. Through my efforts, I made sure every customer was taken care of. The vast majority stayed with us, and as a result, the firm survived.

Nonetheless, I was dogged for many months by the NASD for having insufficient net capital during the crash. They fined me — the only time in forty years I have been fined.

Once I had stabilized the firm and retained a new clearinghouse, I sued my old clearing firm for not properly supervising our clients. I settled for $750,000 and used this money to pay off the loans I had taken to save the firm. We started making money again and continued to do underwriting. But as a result of the crash, I decided to give up my firm's independence and partner with a larger NYSE-member firm, becoming a boutique underwriting division of that firm. There were no capital requirements to do this sort of business. I simply had to pay the expenses of my office. This gave me a chance to get back to my primary expertise, investment banking. In this framework, I continued to do four to six deals a year.

My previous experience at AVTEK taught me that as the major shareholder, I would bear the primary responsibility for my firm's difficulties. But I was still surprised at friends and associates who deserted me during the difficult times, even though they owned a share of the company. They did not think the firm could survive, and they wanted to save themselves.

I came out of this experience wiser and financially

stronger, and with a better understanding of human nature. In a crisis, many people will only think of themselves and will not work for the good of the company. I believe that a person's true strengths and weaknesses come out in a crisis.

Today I own and run Providence Capital Group. We own and operate factories in Massachusetts, North Carolina, and Mexico, primarily in the wire, cable, and cable harness businesses, employing 350 people. We supply original equipment manufacturers and the defense industry with highly specialized, technical products. We also give management and financial advice to firms experiencing difficulties. Sometimes we are appointed by the bankruptcy courts to give advice to such distressed companies. I've learned a lot in my own career that is valuable for other companies to learn.

Deals

I never attempt to make money on the stock market.
I buy on the assumption that they could close the market
the next day and not reopen it for five years.

WARREN BUFFETT
(American businessman, investor, and philanthropist, b. 1930)

Have you ever watched "Shark Tank" on television? People with small- to medium-sized businesses ask rich and powerful entrepreneurs to invest in their companies. The potential investors ask pointed questions and try to get a very favorable deal for giving the small company money. They are very aggressive with their questioning and sometimes fight with each other to grab a good deal. That's why they are "sharks."

I am not a shark (I hope), but I do have a similar ability as those television investors to quickly judge the worth of a business. After taking eighty companies public, I have learned a lot about what makes a business successful. I think one of my greatest strengths is my ability to judge the potential of a company and the people running the company. The following is a small sample of some of the more interesting deals I have done.

RICHMOND SQUARE

The roots of Richmond Square in Providence, Rhode Island, stem from an ambitious project called the Greenhouse Compact. The Greenhouse Compact was developed in the early 1980s to try to get Rhode Island into high tech areas using venture capital money. The idea was to form a sort of Silicon Valley in Rhode Island. There was a bond issue to help get the project going, but it failed because the state's politicians didn't get behind it. It had support from the universities in Rhode Island, but the initiative failed to pass.

In 1984, after the Greenhouse Compact didn't work out, my friend Harold Shine told me about an old mill he wanted to redevelop as an executive park. The site was a turn-of-the-century factory that was classified as historic, with tax savings available for investors. He needed one million dollars to get the project started.

Harold wanted to build the complex as executive offices with shared receptionists and conference rooms. Remembering the Greenhouse Compact, I thought the old mill might be perfect for a business incubator project, a smaller version of what the Greenhouse Compact was trying to accomplish. Harold loved the idea. In addition to the money we borrowed, I put in one million dollars to own half the project and receive all the tax credits.

It cost between four to five million dollars and two years time to complete the renovation. A twelve-foot kiln in the old mill was turned into one of the conference rooms. We made a large entrance area for receptionists and offered printing and other services for all the tenants. Some tenants used the space as executive offices, but most were start-up businesses. For these new companies, we developed the Richmond Square venture fund. Most of our investments in start-up companies were relatively small, but I made a $100,000 investment in at least one company.

The Richmond Square complex had about eighty thousand square feet of space. Roughly one thousand jobs were created by companies that participated in the project. When a new company came in to the incubator project, I would often do a quick analysis on the firm's financials and give the company advice on how to grow.

The Richmond Square project was a success for many of the tenants, and was also rewarding in many ways for me. I received one million dollars in tax credits because of the historic buildings. That tax credit saved me $500,000. After a couple of years, the project started generating positive cash flow. After ten years, my partner Harold bought me out for $1.5 million, and I retained investments in some of the companies that had located in the project.

The Richmond Square project brought a level of sophistication that would not have been available to most entrepreneurs in the area at that time. We helped entrepreneurs understand what they needed to develop a business plan. If the project looked promising, I would arrange for financing and provide advice to the business in its start-up stage.

I think that when we started Richmond Square in 1985, the conditions were more favorable for start-ups than they are today. Now, when someone tells me they have a great idea, I am more likely to tell them to sell their idea to a company that's already in business rather than start a new company. Today it's tougher than it's ever been to get a start-up functioning full speed. To create a business today is difficult financially because marketing and manufacturing are very expensive and raising money is hard for startups. If have an idea or a product that's valuable, it's often better to sell it to an established business.

Even if a start-up company finds investors, there are many pitfalls. There are plenty of sharks in the waters. Many undercapitalized entrepreneurs eventually lose control of their own companies. Investors will often put up more money after their initial investment only if they can assume control. Some venture capitalists put the company in a vulnerable position by withholding promised money, and then put the capital in at the last minute to take control of the company to save it. It's happened hundreds of times on Wall Street. It's a classic move of diluting the existing shareholders (including the founder of the business!) and saying, "You're the old people. We're the new people. We have control over this now."

I liked the opportunity of working with companies with great prospects and taking them public. But the venture capital business became tougher and tougher. Funds for smaller companies dried up. In 1996, seeing the changes in the industry, I left the brokerage business. Because there was too much risk and financing was so tight, I was not comfortable continuing my efforts to finance new companies.

I was not done with investing, however. I decided to concentrate in the turn-around business—working with distressed companies. Such companies have potential, but the current management of those firms may not have the capital or expertise to make the company successful. I can help by bringing new bank financing and management expertise to the project. Adding new ideas and new capital often helps a company find the path to success. Because I took so many companies public, I learned how to deal with a wide variety of businesses.

Today, most active venture investors won't deal with any project that requires less than one million dollars. There's too much risk and not enough reward for venture capitalists to deal with companies that small. It's similar to my experience when I was starting out as a stockbroker. It took just as much effort to make a trade of one hundred shares as it did to make a sale of one thousand shares. And the commission on one thousand shares was ten times as great as the commission on one hundred shares. Venture capitalists think the same way. Why waste time on small deals when they can make so much more money on medium-sized and large deals?

When you have a small company (by small, I mean any company doing less than several million dollars

> If necessary and you really believe in your ideas, borrow against your house or any other collateral you possess. You must first put your own assets up if you want to raise money from other people. If you don't make the commitment to use your own resources first, it's difficult to raise money from anyone else.

a year in sales), my advice to the entrepreneur is to get additional money from family and friends.

A rich uncle can be an invaluable asset. If necessary and you really believe in your ideas, borrow against your house or any other collateral you possess. You must first put your own assets up if you want to raise money from other people. If you don't make the commitment to use your own resources first, it's difficult to raise money from anyone else.

It's very tough to attract other people's money. Banks only give a loan if it's backed by collateral — assets they can take if the loan goes bad. Even substantial inventory in your products is often valued by a bank as nearly or totally worthless. Banks worry that if your business is going under, there may not be new customers for your existing inventory. Banks will discount your goodwill, your assets, even your real estate and accounts receivable. That is why it is so difficult to borrow money from banks. Banks can be helpful when your business is doing well, but don't expect most bankers to have sympathy when your business is in distress.

How does someone with an idea and no money fund a new business? The Small Business Administration (SBA) is one solution. The SBA has been around since 1953, and they have knowledgeable volunteers who can help evaluate a new business. It will take your house as collateral, but the SBA is a good source of money.

> When I am evaluating a company, I try to determine if the owner of a company is competent, realistic, and knowledgeable. Then I look at the product. It has to be something that makes a difference in people's lives and is needed.

Some states have incubator projects to help budding entrepreneurs. For example, Massachusetts has a high-tech fund that is job-based. These state programs may also require collateralizing your house, but such programs are helpful when bank funding is not an option.

Financing alone is not enough. The combination of the right management and the right products enable a company to succeed. I've seen fabulous ideas go nowhere because of the lack of leadership. And I've seen great leadership save companies who were in trouble.

When I am evaluating a company, I try to determine if the owner of a company is competent, realistic, and knowledgeable. Then I look at the product. It has to be something that makes a difference in people's lives and is needed.

MUSIC INVESTMENTS

One important lesson I've learned in my investment career is that you shouldn't get involved in a project unless you make a concerted effort to learn everything about it. Consider two opportunities I had in the music business.

One day in 1974, two young men walked into my Providence office and asked if I was interested in promoting three concerts for a new Boston-area band. I had never heard of the band, but these Brown University seniors made them sound exciting and I figured, why not? I paid $7,500 to stage three concerts for the band. The first gig, in a National Guard armory in Fall River, Massachusetts, on April 21, 1974, was a sellout. When it was over, I received a bill for five hundred dollars to clean up the mess the band left. I decided this was no business for me, so I called local concert promoter Frank Russo, who was a good friend, and asked him to take over the remaining two dates. Which he did. The band happened to be Aerosmith. I made the cardinal mistake in not knowing enough about the musicians I was backing. Seeing lead singer Steven Tyler on *American Idol* recently, I am again reminded of my bad decision! Had I just stuck it out…

But I avoided making another musical mistake through pure luck. Promoter Frank Russo called me with an opportunity to get in on the Jackson's Victory Tour — yes, *those* Jacksons, Michael Jackson and his family, the final reunion tour for the former Jackson Five. Frank said, "This is unbelievable, this is going to be $100-million gross but I need front money." Specifically, he needed $10 million. I made a few calls seeking capital, though not enthusiastically.

Before I had gotten very far, Russo called a few days later and said, "Tom, I got the ten million. I just signed the contract. It's going to be in the newspapers tomorrow." I congratulated him, and thought to myself: *"You just blew one of the best deals of your life."* Here's where the luck comes in — others' bad luck, my good. Two months later the headlines in our local paper said Michael Jackson had fired Russo and he was now taking advice from Don King, the boxing promoter.

King brought in the Sullivan family, who at that time were the owners of the New England Patriots. The Sullivans put up the $10 million in front money, but King kept all the ancillary business (CDs, tee shirts, etc.) for himself. He also had an entourage of dozens added to the payroll. The tour went on, and even though it was one of the highest grossing tours at the time, the Sullivan family lost most of its investment. One of the consequences of the bad investment was that the family was forced to sell the Patriots football team. A few years later Robert Kraft bought the team that has become one of the most lucrative sports franchises in the country.

VISX

One of my more interesting and profitable business ventures had its roots when I was seven years old. My nearsightedness forced me to wear glasses. I hated the glasses because they interfered with sports, but my eyesight was so poor that I had to wear them.

In the early 1980s, I heard about a new optical surgical correction procedure, radial keratotomy. Developed by Russian ophthalmologist Svyatoslav Fyodorov, the procedure had just been approved by the US Food and Drug Administration for use in this country. Dr. Paul S. Koch, an ophthalmologist in Rhode Island, was offering the procedure. I had the radial keratotomy procedure and was thrilled that I no longer had to wear heavy glasses. Koch went on to build a major regional practice, Koch Eye Associates, which is still thriving today.

Not long after my surgery, I was approached by another ophthalmologist, Dr. Francis E. O'Donnell, who trained at Johns Hopkins' Wilmer Eye Institute. Frank was a professor and chairman of the department of ophthalmology at the Saint Louis University School of Medicine. He wanted to provide education to ophthalmologists around the world via satellite. This was a radical idea for the 1980s, long before the emergence of Skype and other means of teleconferencing. Frank had joined forces with an investor, Jonnie R. Williams, one of the most charismatic men I've ever met. I helped them raise a few million dollars and take their small company, Eyesat, public.

We did other deals together, including a biotech company, Mast Therapeutics, Inc. In the mid-1980s, Frank told me about new research into a laser technique to correct vision, an advance over radial keratotomy. An IBM scientist discovered that the excimer laser could be used in ablating tissue one cell at a time. IBM sold the concept to a large corporation, but that company lost interest.

Frank wanted to transform the excimer laser division of the large corporation into a freestanding private company. We arranged the spinoff and the financing, and worked with VISX for years as the company sought FDA approval for its laser machine. Eventually, we took the company public.

At Frank's suggestion, the technology was first offered in Canada, England, and Italy, where government approvals are less stringent than in the United States. We eventually received FDA approval in the United States for the machine, and it was very popular in this country, as well. Years later, VISX was sold to Abbott Medical Optics for over a billion dollars.

Everyone profited nicely, and my eyes are still fine. I haven't worn glasses in years.

LOTUS

I have been a car nut for about as long as I can remember. My first car was a 1951 Mercedes 220, which I bought for $250 in Germany in 1960 while I was in the Army. This began my long love affair with Mercedes and other cars, including Lamborghinis, Lotuses, Jaguars, and Corvettes, in which I raced.

But perhaps my favorite was a 1981 Giugiaro-designed Lotus Turbo Esprit, an extraordinary machine that could go from zero to sixty in 4.3 seconds with a top speed, in fifth gear, of more than 150 miles per hour. Only 173 of these mid-engine marvels were ever produced, and 100 of them came in a deal I helped put together that saved Lotus during the early 1980s.

Lotus was started in 1952 by Colin Chapman, a graduate of University College, London. The company's first factory was housed in old stables behind the Railway Hotel in Hornsey, North London. Since 1966 Lotus has had a factory and road test facility at Hethel, near Wymondham, England.

Only a handful of Lotus cars were sold each year in the United States. By 1982, the company was experiencing severe financial difficulties. Chapman sought additional capital from outside sources. Car enthusiast and Yale Law School professor and investment banker Joe Bianco, who was a good friend of Chapman, came to our firm seeking help.

Joe and our brokers raised the four million dollars needed to save Lotus by selling shares in a new American company, Lotus Performance Cars Inc. For

$100,000 each, forty investors received stock plus a Lotus Turbo Esprit with their name etched in silver on the steering wheel. I bought the first one myself. We made the stock sales, raised the capital, and saved Lotus from bankruptcy.

Sadly, Chapman died in 1982, but his company continued. Its engineering, which had gone into F-1 racers, was so prized that General Motors bought Lotus in 1986. By then, shares we had sold in 1982 earned each investor about $300,000 when the GM sale went through. Not a bad profit. And I ended up with a very fine car, one of my all-time favorites.

BIZ2NET

The year was 1999, the height of the dotcom frenzy.

I received a phone call from Andy Lovelace Evans, who said that he worked with Bill Gates and had an interest in my company Biz2Net. He wanted to fly his personal jet to Rhode Island the next day to talk to me.

Biz2Net was a company I bought out of bankruptcy and had nurtured for many years. I was the chairman of the board and Biz2Net's largest stockholder. The company had developed software that enabled businesses to fulfill orders on their websites. Biz2Net was doing about ten million dollars in sales per year. We had been advised by Bache and Co. that the value of Biz2Net could be as high as one hundred million dollars, although we were aware that market valuations for Internet companies were volatile and thought a more conservative valuation was appropriate. Bache wanted us to raise ten to fifteen million dollars privately before taking us public, so our investment banker H. C. Wainright put together a proposal, which had found its way to Andy Evans. I checked on Evans and I found out that he was handling Bill Gates' personal investments and that Bill Gates was the godfather to all three of Evans's children.

I arranged to pick up Evans at the private airport at Quonset Point the next day. I met with him all day and he had dinner with my wife and me. Evans wove an incredible story how he had been friends with Bill Gates for many years and was the owner of a brokerage firm that was destined to take Microsoft public, but Microsoft had grown so fast they decided they needed a major firm to put together the deal. He lived on an island off the coast of Washington and ran a company called Zero.net.

Evans thought the dotcom craze was just starting and he was putting together a group of companies to take advantage of it. He had signed a deal to acquire a cosmetics company, Perfumania. Evans's plan was to acquire more Internet companies, and Biz2Net was to be the key company. Its management would be in charge of his whole company.

It was agreed that in exchange for a one million dollar loan, we would sell our company to Perfumania for $40 million in Perfumania stock. This was lower than Bache's $100 million evaluation, but we felt the more conservative figure was safer for an Internet company.

This transaction was finalized in November 1999. I thought that we were about to cash in on one of our biggest hits. By this time, I was fairly cynical about the machinations of certain Wall Street promoters, but this deal sounded interesting enough to inform my directors, the management team, and investors. We signed a binding agreement with Perfumania, received the one million dollars, and Evans put two members on our board.

Everyone was ecstatic about the deal and thought it was the quickest way to cash in on what was turning out to be a terrific investment. The board and investors were constantly calling me to know when the closing would take place. Perfumania stock was moving up almost on a daily basis and if we closed in January, the deal would be worth $80 million. But as January 2000 came to an end, it became more and more difficult to reach Evans.

One Monday morning in early February 2000, I got a call from the president of Biz2Net, telling me that twenty of the key staff members had not shown up for work.

In the next few days, we found that Evans had bought a smaller company in Massachusetts in a similar business for substantially less than the price he had agreed to pay for Biz2Net. He enticed our key employees with front money and stock to move over to his new firm, Envision Development Company.

We sued, and we agreed to settle for eleven million dollars in Envision stock with registration rights. But before we could complete the transaction, the Envision stock crashed and was selling for pennies a share. Today, the stock sits in my office safe as a reminder how potential profits can sometimes be very fleeting.

COLD FUSION

In 1989 two scientists at the University of Utah, Stanley Pons and Martin Fleischmann, claimed to have made a breakthrough in what became known as "cold fusion." Traditional science assumed you would need extremely high temperatures and pressure to create fusion. There were a lot of skeptics, but the pair had some high-profile advocates, including Ira Magaziner from Rhode Island, who worked on the state's Greenhouse Compact and was a senior policy advisor for President Bill Clinton.

Magaziner, Pons, and Fleischmann made a proposal before the Science Committee of the House of Representatives for a $25 million investment by the government in the new technology. Congress didn't approve the investment, but it sparked interest in the technology around the world. I thought that if Ira Magaziner backed it, I should check it out. I went to Salt Lake City and was shown the cold fusion experiments. I was convinced of the value of cold fusion. We created Eneco Inc. and purchased the patent rights for the technology from the University of Utah to develop and patent the technology around the world.

I became the financial adviser to the company

and ended up investing nearly a million dollars of my own money and raised millions from investors. Soon I was off to international conferences on cold fusion in Monte Carlo and Vancouver. One night I found myself sitting next to former astronaut Buzz Aldrin at dinner and next day I was meeting scientists from all over the world. This was heady stuff for me.

After ten years and at least $25 million invested, there were still many doubts about the technology. Eneco came to realize that commercialization could be many years off, if ever, and turned its efforts to other ways to improve energy efficiency. I moved on, too.

Today there are dozens of scientists at labs around the world still working to develop cold fusion technology. Their motto is "Forty billion dollars and forty years have been spent on hot fusion, so why not a similar effort in cold fusion?" One thing is for sure: the last word on cold fusion has not been written.

PART TWO

What I Learned on the Roller Coaster

Wall Street

The individual incentive not to commit crime on Wall Street now is almost zero.

MATT TAIBBI
(American journalist, b. 1970)

Wall Street has always been, and always will be, an insider's game. Greed and ego drive the action on Wall Street. There are a lot of honest and hard-working people on Wall Street, but the trading pits and investment houses are filled with people who only care about making money.

When I worked on Wall Street, I was the lead or sole underwriter in over eighty initial public offerings (IPOs). Almost all were early-stage companies that used new capital from underwritings to create and expand jobs. The people at the top made handsome profits, but ordinary Joes also benefitted.

My specialty was technology companies, and as a former engineer, I was far more up-to-date on new technology than those with only financial backgrounds or MBAs. Most of the companies I took public are still stand-alone enterprises or have merged into larger companies. Thousands of jobs were created as these companies grew.

During this period, I learned that Wall Street greed could be contained. The regulators did their work, and Wall Street firms did a pretty good job of supervising staff. But firms were beginning to rely on computer trading in the 1980s, and the mechanization of trading actually made systems more unreliable.

The dangers of computer trading became apparent during the market crash of 1987, when many people realized that the system had serious flaws that could not prevent quick major moves in the market, up or down. The effects of computerizing every aspect of trading made large moves more common. But the genie had been let out of the bottle and there was no turning back. Computerization had made blow-ups more common, but the profitability of massive amounts of computer trading makes it unlikely that the good old days of non-machine trading will ever return. Today, the firms with the fastest computers have an edge over other firms and individual traders, often with milliseconds making the difference.

Wall Street underwriting used to be about capitalizing companies and creating jobs. Now I think it seems to be about creating jobs and profit for Wall Street insiders.

Some on Wall Street seem to be playing "heads I win, tails you lose." Because individual traders have to pay much higher fees and commissions than the big firms, individuals who do too much trading might be better off in a casino. The odds are stacked against them when they go up against the big boys and fast computers of Wall Street.

SHORT SALES

Among the insiders, the Wall Street money managers, there are two types of players: those who belong to what is called the buy side (the much larger group) and those who belong to the sell side. The buy side, or the longs, invest in those equities they think will appreciate. The sell side, the shorts, try to profit from companies they think will depreciate in value. The shorts do this by selling shares they do not own, in companies that they think are overpriced. They then will be able to cover their shorts by buying the stock at a lower price.

I believe that the current rules favor the shorts. If you believe in a company and its future, you have to be very careful in putting out any good information, as it will be scrutinized by lawyers and the SEC for its accuracy, and you risk class action lawsuits if you make a misstatement. However, if you are on the short side, you can put out misleading information without fear, and use any devious method to reduce the price of a security. There is no penalty for disparaging a stock by giving your opinion that it is overpriced or worthless. I think it's a similar offense to promote a stock by lying, or to push the price down by putting out erroneous information. But current regulations do not punish the shorts for misinformation.

There are constant battles between shorts and longs on Wall Street. Short sellers do not own stock they sell. The short sellers borrow the stock, sell it, and receive money for it. At some time in the future, the short sellers have to buy back the stock. If the stock is at a lower price when they buy it back, the short sellers make money. Basically, short sellers are betting that the price of a stock will go down.

I personally believe dishonesty on Wall Street is most often found among the short sellers. I have been in a number of battles between the shorts and longs as an underwriter, always on the long side. I have found out just how dirty the shorts will fight to protect their positions.

Suppose a biotech company has no revenues but it has a potential billion-dollar drug that can cure some disease. Waiting for FDA approval can take years and millions of dollars. Typically, the company needs additional funds to carry it through the approval process, which is very expensive. The shorts see this as a ripe opportunity to make a profit and will put out bogus stories at critical times to depress the stock price. When the stock goes down, the shorts make a profit. The lower the price of the stock, the bigger the profit for the shorts. Using an army of bloggers and newsletters offered over the Internet, the shorts will make the case that the company may not get FDA approval. They say investing in the company is too risky, while at the same time selling borrowed shares to depress the price further. The game plan of short sellers is to make

Tom DePetrillo with his wife, Carol Keefe, Esq.

DePetrillo children, c. 1947.
Frank, Eleanor, Nick, Tom, Larry, Carol, Linda (l. to r.)

Frank DePetrillo with his invention,
the scroll machine, c. 1949.

CLOCKWISE FROM TOP LEFT

Tom, c.1950

DePetrillo siblings, c. 1951. Tom, Carol, Larry (l. to r.)

Tom as an Army Specialist Fourth Class, working on missile systems.

A few prospectuses of the over eighty venture capital deals Tom has handled.

Sullivan Stadium, home field of the New England Patriots, c. 1972 (note Tom's company, AVTEK, on the score board).

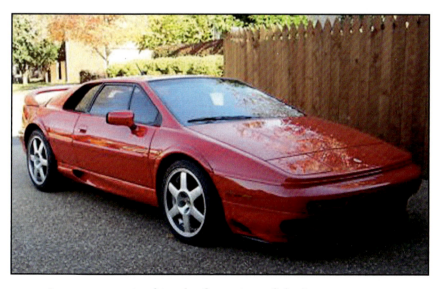

Lotus car received in the financing of the Lotus company.

Tom's Cable Assembly plant in Whitsett, North Carolina.

A view of the wire and cable manufacturing facility.

Are pharmaceuticals more valuable than gold?

Tom DePetrillo with President Barack Obama

the shares look weak to panic others into selling. Then the shorts buy those shares back at a lower price to cover their position and make a profit. The shorts have no concern about the impact on the company, which because its stock has fallen in price, may have lost out on the chance to raise money at a fair market price. If the shorts put out false information, a drug may not come to market and society may have lost a chance at curing a disease.

I fought a battle with short sellers when I was helping underwrite the laser vision company VISX. The shorts put out many stories that no legitimate ophthalmologist would ever shine a high-power laser into someone's eyes. Today, thousands of ophthalmologists do just that (now called LASIK) to millions of patients.

TOO BIG TO FAIL

Most people are familiar with fantasy football and fantasy baseball. The rules are simple: assemble a team from among all of the players in the National Football League or Major League Baseball and pretend that this group is actually a team. Take the statistics from each player, use them as if they were on this make-believe team and see how the fantasy team would have done during the actual major-league season. The winner is the fantasy-league participant who picked the best group of players. It's all for fun (and maybe a few dollars wagered).

But there was a comparable game on Wall Street.

It was a real game, with real stakes, that only a few privileged people could play.

I like to call it "fantasy Wall Street."

Wall Street insiders call it "the derivative market."

Derivatives are securities that are based on the price of other assets. They were developed centuries ago to give traders a way to protect themselves against the rise and fall of commodities such as rice and wheat.

Recently, derivatives were developed on intangible assets such as mortgages. A pool of mortgages was created and the pool was given a rating by agencies such as Moody's or Standard & Poor's. These new derivatives had no assets but were backed up by the underlying mortgages. Firms such as Lehman Brothers and Goldman Sachs then sold the new product to institutional and private investors. One of the problems was that the ratings agencies were paid by the firms such as Lehman Brothers and Goldman Sachs to rate the derivatives. The firms pressured the ratings agencies to give high ratings so they could sell these products to their customers. It turned out that ratings were incredibly wrong. The derivatives funds crashed when the housing bubble burst in 2007 and 2008.

The government stepped in and bailed out many of the banks and investment companies putting together these kinds of derivative products, firms that were in the government's estimation, "too big to fail."

In my opinion, these derivatives did not really advance our economy but rather, were developed to feed more money into the Wall Street trading engine.

The value of these artificial products was huge, and Wall Street firms did not have enough capital to survive a severe market downturn in the securities underpinning the products. The whole enterprise was "Fantasy Wall Street," a game not unlike "Fantasy Football" but with far more danger to our economy. When the government decided to bail out the big banks and investment houses, Wall Street ended up okay, but the country as a whole suffered.

It wasn't so long ago that Wall Street was the engine of the economy — the place where companies were born, jobs were created, and the economy was energized. That's all changed. Today, it's mostly all about transactions or trading, where most of the wealth that's created is concentrated in the hands of the traders and their wealthy clients.

Every day, millions of trades are done on Wall Street: stocks, bonds, and other financial instruments such as options and derivatives. True, there are still initial public offerings, the sale of stocks to create or expand companies that actually provide jobs and contribute to the growth of the overall economy. But so much of Wall Street activity now is between and among traders. Most of the jobs that are created are jobs for more Wall Street traders.

All this activity is a zero-sum game. The net contribution to America's economy is zero.

Here's another way to think about this: You have a one hundred dollar investment. Imagine that two firms were trading your investment with each other and each took a one dollar commission on each trade. After fifty trades, the firms would have all your money. That's why most investors should stay away from excess trading, because it eats away at your capital.

I applaud investment and management firms like Warren Buffett's Berkshire Hathaway that give their clients solid long-term returns. Certain mutual funds and pension investment plans are good deals for the average investor. The managers of these funds are mostly honorable people, providing a service and taking a small commission for their hard work.

Why do the best and brightest from our top educational institutions head to Wall Street firms? As Willy Sutton said about robbing banks, "That's where the money is." And some of these newly minted financial types work for firms with the same ethics as Willy.

People who have the opportunity to make a lot of money quickly often only think about their personal wealth, not the impact of their decisions on other people or society in general. Big financial institutions are not charities and must be profitable to survive. But our society has to understand the impact of big firms' financial decisions on people's lives and our country's economy.

The near collapse of the financial system in 2008-2009 was the result of insufficient regulation. Egos and greed had spun out of control. There were some good guys in the Wild West atmosphere of the beginning years of the 21st century. The good guys were the regulators and independent analysts and investigators who tried to expose the egregious activities of some of

Wall Street's players. The real heroes were people like Harry Markopoulos and Elizabeth Warren who investigated Wall Street excesses and shady practices. But these truth-tellers were stymied in their efforts to make fundamental changes in our system. The big money players won out in the end.

> If the big boys on Wall Street have the inside track on something, most people should get out of their way. You don't want to bet against house money.

The winners were the one percent at the highest end of the compensation schedule. Many of them were working at firms that were deemed by our government "too big to fail." The losers in this Wall Street tragedy were the millions who lost their homes or their savings or their retirement accounts. So while the "99 percent" suffered foreclosures and loss of retirement savings, the biggest traders on Wall Street survived and prospered.

The emergence of protests against Wall Street and big banks came as no surprise to me. I was surprised that they did not happen sooner.

All investments have risks, especially for the ordinary citizen. But companies labeled "too big to fail" were somehow insulated from making horrendous market decision. I am upset they haven't jailed one person from the last crash. The fallout from the crash caused the government hundreds of billions of dollars and the government hasn't prosecuted anyone yet.

Here's my theory on why nothing happened. Too many people were involved. Can you put half of Wall Street in jail? The government decided to save the economy and not worry about the people that caused it. It may have made a bad situation worse if the government had tried to prosecute all the villains in the crash of 2008. They rescued the big players and increased the FDIC protection from $100,000 to $250,000 to bolster the public's confidence in their deposits and prevent a run on banks.

In general, if the big boys on Wall Street have the inside track on something, most people should get out of their way. You don't want to bet against house money.

TECHICAL ANALYSIS VS. FUNDAMENTALS

There are financial pundits who are fond of speaking a lot without saying anything helpful. These are the ones who speak in more vague terms, such as, "the market is trending up." Trending up for how long? A day? A week? A month? One of my favorite dubious sayings is: "While short-term positions may remain volatile, the long term looks positive." What exactly does that mean? It's pure doublespeak. The best at this type of vacuous talk are the technical analysts, who say something like this:

"If the markets move up more than five percent,

thereby breaking through a bull technical resistance line, the market will have a further move up. If the market goes down more than five percent, it will have broken through a bear resistance line and will go down further." There's very little helpful information about market direction in that type of doublespeak.

But there is a need for legitimate market analysis. A huge fund management firm like Fidelity Investments, which handles trillions of dollars, employs a virtual army of legitimate analysts. These people can help individual consumers make rational choices about individual stocks and stock funds.

Some players in the stock market rely on technical analysis, based primarily on its stock — its volume, and the change in its stock over time. The use of computers has made technical analysis a very popular way of trading, particularly for day traders. Technical analysts believe that the stock price tells you all you need to know when trading, or, to look at it another way, the market price reflects the true value of a company as reflected by all the buyers and sellers who have determined its price. Technical analysts have a catchy saying: "The trend is your friend." Change in share price is thus very important data for technical analysts.

But these analysts often ignore a stock's fundamentals, which I believe is more important. Researching a company is much more difficult than just following its price, but that effort has paid off for me over the years. Fundamental analysis attempts to weed out some of the emotion that can accompany trading by focusing in on the underlying prospects of a business.

Analyzing a company's fundamentals involves examining its financial statements, its earnings and market capitalization, the depth and expertise of its management, its competitive edge, its competitors, the relative strength of its industry, and where and how it makes and sells its goods or services. Fundamental analysis requires knowledge of the economy, including such indicators as interest rates and employment figures. Fundamental analysis basically requires you to become a "student" of a firm and of the overall economy. The market price is part of that calculation—but only a part.

I met a very successful day trader at a dinner party in Florida. He was a wealthy man who said he expected to make $20,000 to $30,000 a month from trading. "What's your secret?" I asked.

"For years, I was a technical trader," he said. "I did the charts and everything else. Then one day I woke up and realized I wasn't making money. So I decided to do the opposite of what everyone else was doing, I went against the herd mentality. When other technical traders were saying buy, I sold. And when the herd was saying sell, I bought." He ended up making much more by fighting the trend than following it.

Some people do have a knack for trading by just following prices. But I will stick to the fundamentals — unless I'm betting against the herd.

LETTING EMPLOYEES GO

Following the blow-up on Wall Street in 2007 and 2008, our country entered a period called the "Great Recession." In the current stagnation, we hear frequently of corporate acquisitions in which the new owners of company come in and let people go as part of the turnaround process. Often, employees who are fired like this show up at work one day, are escorted into a room, and told to clear out their things immediately. People let go often receive no severance pay, no promise of references, not even a "thank you."

I don't question the need to trim a labor force as a way back toward profitability. I have been involved in turnarounds where I had to let people go. Sometimes it's the only way a company can restore profitability.

In a situation where people have to lose jobs, there is a right way, a humane way, to accomplish the goal.

In my turnarounds, I have always treated people with dignity. I have provided severance packages and references. I have given encouragement and I have always been respectful of the contributions of employees who had to lose their jobs.

> In a situation where people have to lose jobs, there is a right way, a humane way, to accomplish the goal.

INVESTMENT TIPS

From my experience, day trading, market timing, and exotic financial instruments are not appropriate for most people. They are like the big wheel at the casino, a lot of excitement with really poor odds.

So how should ordinary people invest their earnings? They should invest in mutual funds from firms with good track records. Most people should not be in the stock market with their own investment strategy. Wall Street is an inside game and you can't beat someone who spends sixty hours a week working on Wall Street with access to lots of information, fast computers, and low transaction costs.

My advice for most people is not to try to actively manage your own portfolio. Unless you're willing to pay your dues on Wall Street, leave the investing to professionals. You need a solid, conservative market professional on your side.

How about real estate as a way for people to invest? Since we're still climbing out a major recession, could this be the perfect time to buy a distressed property and rent it out? Perhaps. But there is a management side to real estate. Suppose you buy a house that once sold for $300,000 and buy it for the discounted price of $150,000.

It costs $1,200 a month for a mortgage and you rent it for $2,000 a month. Sounds like a good deal, doesn't it? But what if the renter doesn't pay the rent? It takes a few months to get the renter out and the meantime he may have trashed the house and it will cost $50,000 to fix it. Real estate requires hands-on, day-to-day management.

If you're well off and looking for a second home in Florida, now could be a great time to buy a great house or condo at a huge discount. In addition, mortgage rates are low right now. But real estate as an investment usually doesn't work out unless you are in the real estate business.

Government

*It is to be regretted that the rich and powerful
too often bend the acts of government
to their own selfish purposes.*
ANDREW JACKSON
(7th US president, 1767-1845)

Government can be a tremendous force for good in our society. It is not only a safety net and a mechanism to defend our country, but it can also help businesses and the economy grow. Government regulations can also help insure that businesses operate honestly and in an environmentally safe fashion.

The government was a tremendous help to me early in my business career. When I first started out, I received Small Business Administration (SBA) loans, a program supported by the federal government, which helps small businesses obtain loans through their local banks. Despite having to put up collateral such as a house, the loan program has helped many thousands of businesses get started. These businesses wouldn't quality for ordinary bank loans without the help of this federal program.

As I became more financially secure, I no longer

needed the SBA loan program, and I started working with banks directly. Banks may also require collateral but bank loans have fewer restrictions and paperwork.

When I started to work with large companies, government regulations and government contracts became a major factor in my business life. I do a lot of military business in one of my companies. We do a quality job, it's a profitable business, and it never goes overseas. Military contracting and programs are important for a wide variety of companies, and military bases are the linchpins of many city governments.

ENFORCING RULES

Despite what some critics say, governmental regulations can be helpful to society. The government can protect your property, your business, and your finances by enforcing common sense rules.

In some countries without real regulations, businesses can be run in ways that put workers at great risk for sickness or injury. There is no comprehensive safety system in Russia or China, for example. If you're in Nigeria and you have a profitable mining operation, the government can shut down your business because tit wants to take it over, and you can't do anything about it.

Our legal system helps many of our businesses succeed. To insure that business and the public are protected, our country needs regulations both to help businesses get started and to protect them once they are in operation.

LOCAL POLITICS

The Republicans want all our problems to be solved on the state or local level. They claim that local governments are far closer to local problems and can solve them without interference from Washington. But sometimes the local political system is broken. Kickbacks and cheating can be difficult to erase on the local level. Many local officials have been indicted for taking bribes or receiving payments from contractors. If the local government has too much power, there is a greater incidence of corruption.

In addition to corruption, there is also inefficiency. In the state of Rhode Island, we have thirty-nine towns. So we have thirty-nine school principals. We have thirty-nine different bureaucracies to run those thirty-nine schools. Local control can be very costly. If schools were regionalized, the school districts and the state could save money because the schools would require fewer administrators and regulators.

In addition to inefficiencies of scales, many municipalities and state governments have financially unfeasible deals for employee pensions. Many people blame the unions, but I think the true blame lies not just with municipal unions but also with the politicians who agreed to unreasonable union contracts. Some unions have persuaded politicians who were either corrupt or uninformed to put our cities and states in the pension binds they are now in.

PRIVATIZING PRISONS

Republicans talk a lot about privatizing government functions. Their reasoning is that private companies can work more efficiently than the government. But there are some tasks that are just not appropriate for private companies. In particular, I am concerned about the privatization of prisons.

Here are two examples of what can happen when a government function, running prisons, is outsourced.

One: A former juvenile court judge in Pennsylvania, Mark Ciavarella, was sentenced to prison for an crime that is difficult to comprehend in its callousness. He accepted a "finder's fee" for sending children, some of them guilty of minor or questionable charges and some actually innocent, to a privately built and operated for-profit juvenile detention center. In all, the prosecutors said, he pocketed nearly one million dollars. This judge sent many children unnecessarily through the criminal detention system so he could get a kickback. This is the type of tragedy that can happen when we outsource functions that government should be doing.

Two: In my home state of Rhode Island we have a privately run federal prison where a notorious incident took place. The prison was holding a foreign national because his visa had expired. He complained of stomach pains for many weeks with no one offering to help. He eventually died in prison of stomach cancer having never seen a doctor. The federal government eventually settled with the family for a large sum and replaced the company running the prison.

EMPATHY

Many conservatives not only want to outsource important government programs, they want to eliminate other programs that really help people.

Many of these budget-cutters would offer to help a sick child, or a hungry and homeless person if they knew those people personally. And yet, many of these same people who are personally compassionate will vote for political candidates who want to cut funding for child health care programs or close soup kitchens and homeless shelters.

Many people think they are acting morally because they gave their used clothes to a local charity, or delivered toys to needy families at Christmas. That certainly helps. But many of these same people cannot see that giving food stamps or heating assistance to the needy is also a necessary part of the social compact.

This lack of empathy occurs because people are attracted to a theory of capitalism that says everyone has to take care of things by themselves. A democracy is a system in which all people may be born with the same rights, but all people are not born equally in terms of finances, health, and intelligence. A true democracy balances people's circumstances so those in need are helped, and those who can succeed without help are able to do so under a protective but not too intrusive government.

Sometimes private sources can take care of these needs, but our government's role is more essential, broad-based, and fair.

> Real empathy comes from concern for all those in need, not just the ones that go to our church or club, or that we see face-to-face. Most of us may not be able to do much on our own to help in a national disaster, or help eradicate poverty in our country, but we can approve effective programs that help those in need.

Real empathy comes from concern for all those in need, not just the ones that go to our church or club, or that we see face-to-face. Most of us may not be able to do much on our own to help in a national disaster, or help eradicate poverty in our country, but we can approve effective programs that help those in need.

SOCIAL SECURITY

Social Security and Medicare have been cornerstones of American public policy for decades. Generations of people have relied on them. By almost any measure, they have been among the most successful initiatives our country has undertaken. These programs have improved the lives of millions of older Americans.

And yet, in recent election cycles, we heard about plans to radically change both programs. Nearly all of the Republican candidates in the last Presidential election urged a radical transformation of both Social Security and Medicare. That sentiment crystallized in the nomination of Mitt Romney and his selection of Wisconsin Congressman Paul Ryan as his running mate. Ryan built his career on the philosophy of downsizing the federal government — gutting might not be too strong a word — and of remaking two treasured programs, Social Security and Medicare. The Republican proposals, I believe, would imperil both.

Although specifics were lacking, the general outlines of what the Romney/Ryan Republicans wanted to do are contained in the 2012 Republican Party national platform. Addressing Medicare and the related Medicaid program, which primarily serves the disabled, the party wrote:

> "The first step is to move the two programs away from their current unsustainable defined-benefit entitlement model to a fiscally sound defined-contribution model. . . . We can do this without making any changes for those 55 and older. While retaining the option of traditional Medicare in competition with private plans, we call for a transition to a premium-support model for Medicare, with an income-adjusted contribution toward a health plan of the enrollee's choice."

For people under the age of 55, this is saying, basically, "Good luck." I don't think the private sector will have the same concern for people's health and well-being as the federal government has since 1965, when President Johnson and Congress united to create Medicare, one of LBJ's greatest Great Society measures.

Should we rely on the private sector for something as critical as health care? Hasn't our recent experience with the worst recession since the Great Depression taught us anything? Is the Medicare "voucher" system the Republicans propose really anything more than a code word for "dismantle?"

London School of Economics scholar Noam Schimmel wrote about Ryan's proposal in a blistering critique on the *Huffington Post* (posted September 4, 2012). Ryan, Schimmel wrote, "is banking on the idea that senior citizens are selfish and only care about their own well-being, and don't have in mind the welfare of their children and grandchildren as well. It's a cynical and misguided assumption." A similar sort of misguided thinking surrounds the Republicans' assessment of Social Security, created by Franklin D. Roosevelt and Congress in 1935, at the height of the Great Depression. In the words of the Republican Party in its 2012 platform:

> "While no changes should adversely affect any current or near-retiree, comprehensive reform should address our society's remarkable medical advances

in longevity and allow younger workers the option of *creating their own personal investment accounts* (emphasis mine) as supplements to the system. Younger Americans have lost all faith in the Social Security system, which is understandable when they read the non-partisan actuary's reports about its future funding status. Born in an old industrial era beyond the memory of most Americans, it is long overdue for major change, not just another legislative stopgap that postpones a day of reckoning. To restore public trust in the system, Republicans are committed to setting it on a sound fiscal basis that will give workers *control over, and a sound return on, their investments* (again, emphasis mine). The sooner we act, the sooner those close to retirement can be reassured of their benefits and younger workers can take responsibility for planning their own retirement decades from now."

What does this mean? Essentially, play the stock market and hope it doesn't crash. Rely on the vicissitudes of Wall Street, not the solemn word of Uncle Sam.

In attempting to sell this nonsense, Romney and Ryan deliberately distorted the truth. I'll give just one example. In accepting his party's vice presidential nomination at Tampa, Ryan accused the Affordable Care Act of taking money from the Medicare program "at the expense of the elderly."

Sounded like a scare tactic. And it was.

According to the respected truth-assessment organization Factcheck, an initiative of the Annenberg Public Policy Center, "In fact, Medicare's chief actuary says the law 'substantially improves' the system's finances, and Ryan himself has embraced the same savings. . . . As we have written many times, the law does not slash the current Medicare budget by $500 billion. Rather, that's a $500 billion reduction in the future growth of Medicare over 10 years, or about a seven percent reduction in growth over the decade. In other words, Medicare spending would continue to rise, just not as much. The law stipulates that guaranteed Medicare benefits won't be reduced, and it adds some new benefits, such as improved coverage for pharmaceuticals."

In one way or another, these Chicken Little arguments and shameless scare tactics have been around for a very long time. Politicians for several decades have declared that the sky is falling on Social Security and Medicare, and if we don't radically change things, both programs will collapse.

Not true. Despite changing demographics (a growing and aging population) and up-and-down economic circumstances, Congress and the President have always found a way to adjust both programs to ensure their survival and health.

The election of 2012 showed that voters believed the radical changes the Republicans wanted to make in these trusted programs were not in the best interest of the average American. Social Security and Medicare do face challenges as the baby boom generation continues to age. Both programs *do* need our attention, as both major political parties agree (one of the few issues on which they do agree).

In their 2012 annual report, the Social Security and Medicare Boards of Trustees, headed by Timothy F. Geithner, Secretary of the Treasury, presented the public with their analysis:

> "Social Security and Medicare are the two largest federal programs, accounting for 36 percent of federal expenditures in fiscal year 2011. Both programs will experience cost growth substantially in excess of GDP growth in the coming decades due to aging of the population and, in the case of Medicare, growth in expenditures per beneficiary exceeding growth in per capita GDP. Through the mid-2030s, population aging caused by the large baby-boom generation entering retirement and lower-birth-rate generations entering employment will be the largest single factor causing costs to grow more rapidly than GDP."

The trustees, including Kathleen Sebelius, Secretary of Health and Human Services, and Hilda L. Solis, Secretary of Labor, urged Congress to take action.

"Lawmakers should not delay addressing the long-run financial challenges facing Social Security and Medicare," they wrote in their 2012 report. "If they take action sooner rather than later, more options and more time will be available to phase in changes so that the public has adequate time to prepare. Earlier action will also help elected officials minimize adverse impacts on vulnerable populations, including lower-income workers and people already dependent on program benefits."

So what do the Democrats offer? In two words: *solutions* and continued *security*.

"We believe every American deserves a secure, healthy, and dignified retirement. America's seniors have earned their Medicare and Social Security through a lifetime of hard work and personal responsibility," wrote the party in its 2012 national platform.

> "During their working years, Americans contribute to Social Security in exchange for a promise that they will receive an income in retirement. Unlike those in the other party, we will find a solution to protect Social Security for future generations. We will block Republican efforts to subject Americans' guaranteed retirement income to the whims of the stock

market through privatization. We reject approaches that insist that cutting benefits is the only answer.

"The Republican budget plan would end Medicare as we know it. Democrats adamantly oppose any efforts to privatize or voucherize Medicare; unlike our opponents we will not ask seniors to pay thousands of dollars more every year while they watch the value of their Medicare benefits evaporate. Democrats believe that Medicare is a sacred compact with our seniors. Nearly 50 million older Americans and Americans with disabilities rely on Medicare each year, and the new health care law makes Medicare stronger by adding new benefits, fighting fraud, and improving care for patients. . . . President Obama is already leading the most successful crackdown on health care fraud ever, having already recovered $10 billion from health care scams. We will build on those reforms, not eliminate Medicare's guarantees."

The Democratic platform did not include detail. But Democratic lawmakers and analysts have provided it in other places. The Affordable Care Act addresses

Medicare. And viable possibilities for Social Security include changing the cost of living calculation; implementing means-testing, so that wealthy people who have no need of government help will stay out of the system; raising the retirement age, not unreasonable, given how people live longer these days; raising the payroll tax cap; or some combination of all.

These challenges are no greater than those that we, as Americans, have faced many times before. And we have always solved them. The only difference now is the gridlock that right-wing Republicans like Ryan and his Tea Party allies have created in Washington.

In accepting his party's presidential nomination in Charlotte, President Obama made a promise to the American people.

"I will never turn Medicare into a voucher," he said, to thunderous applause. "No American should ever have to spend their golden years at the mercy of insurance companies. They should retire with the care and the dignity they have earned. Yes, we will reform and strengthen Medicare for the long haul, but we'll do it by reducing the cost of health care, not by asking seniors to pay thousands of dollars more. And we will keep the promise of Social Security by taking the responsible steps to strengthen it, not by turning it over to Wall Street."

Since 1935, Social Security has been one of the federal government's best-managed and funded programs. Contrary to what some claim, it has no impact on the deficit since employers and employees fund it. In fact, it reduces the cost of government since its excess funds are used to buy US treasuries, thereby lowering the interest charges the government has to pay.

My advice is to leave the fundamentals of Social Security and Medicare in place, but to adjust some of the parameters of the program to deal with our aging population.

EDUCATION POLICY

If we're going to continue to compete successfully with other countries, we need to fix what we're doing wrong with education policy in this country.

We're not doing enough teaching for specific occupations.

After getting a basic education, many high school graduates with technical aptitude would be better off learning certain technical occupations where there is plenty of opportunity, but too often, they don't even know that path could be open to them.

We're not encouraging businesses to educate their employees.

I was lucky to grow up at a time when my employers enhanced and encouraged my education. There's not enough of that going on right now. Everybody's counting on our schools, and our schools don't always teach the special skills our students need in different professions.

We're not doing a good job of meeting the needs of kids like me who don't respond to the structure of school.

Instead of fitting square pegs into round holes, we have to adjust the system to meet the needs of our students. The Theil Fellowship awards $100,000 to kids who don't go to college and work on exciting projects instead. Started by Peter Theil, one of the founders of PayPal, the fellowship program is an interesting way to help young people who want to follow a different road.

We're challenging our public education system on several fronts that don't make sense to me: charter schools, for-profit schools, and home schooling.

I'm not a fan of private companies that are rivals to public education. In the last several years, in many parts of the country, there has been a strong movement to open charter schools, private schools that are publicly-financed institutions and promise to produce certain results, such as a superior academic education or training in the arts. Supporters of charter schools want to obtain relief from local mandates, laws, and teacher's unions.

But teacher standards can be lower in charter schools than in public schools. In Texas, for example, the only qualification to teach at a charter school is a high school diploma. In some charter schools, corporal punishment is allowed; in some, graduation standards are so lax that college admission can be difficult or impossible. Some charter schools focus on discounting scientifically accepted theories such as evolution or climate change. Many charter schools focus on teaching religion or discourage diversity by separating their students from schools serving minority communities.

This flow of dollars out of public schooling toward charter schools is a grave threat to the success of public schools, which is where most American children still receive their primary and secondary educations. Public schools used to be the melting pot for all citizens and immigrants. They are one of the main ingredients of America's greatness. With the advent of charter schools catering to specific types of students, public education is being balkanized. A strong public school system is more American than a charter school with a private agenda.

Charter schools that undermine the "melting pot" value of public school education are not the only threat to the success of our nation's educational system. For-profit Internet-based colleges are, in my opinion, a bad educational idea. While I certainly believe in the profit motive, many for-profit colleges take advantage of financial programs to help students. They profit by exploiting well-intentioned government loan programs that were meant to benefit students, not corporations. They often land students in significant debt without corresponding benefits. In many cases, the owners of the schools make a lot of money while students flounder in debt and the federal government can't be repaid.

One for-profit school in the Midwest was nationally accredited and had about five hundred students when a group of venture capitalists from California bought it a few years ago. The national accreditation allowed students to qualify for government-guaranteed student loans and for Pell Grants (established by the late Rhode Island senator Claiborne Pell, whose campaigns I always supported).

In a few years, the student population grew to 35,000 — almost all taught over the Internet. The owners are earning hundreds of millions of dollars, but has the college helped the students? Many of the students at that college do not graduate and many students are unable to pay back their student loans and then default. The ones that *do* complete their Internet courses and graduate have an almost worthless piece of paper and up to $60,000 in loans that they can't afford. They cannot get jobs, since most employers know that despite having a diploma, the students have not learned the skills needed for the job.

In general, when it comes to Internet-based for-profit colleges, the buyer should be wary. When the prime motivation for an educational institution becomes making money, some owners are unfortunately inclined to deceive their customers — in this case, their students. For-profit colleges are motivated to attract and keep students, and they are not always motivated to help students succeed.

I have been interested in the issue of for-profit colleges for many years. I've watched with some trepidation as the number of for-profit students have grown. For-profit schools have been advertising their programs extensively, especially on cable television and online. The schools get the attention of younger people who may lack the sophistication to make a thoughtful choice about college.

The National Bureau of Economic Research issued a report in December 2011 entitled, "The For-Profit Postsecondary School Sector: Nimble Critters or Agile Predators?" written by three well-respected scholars: David J. Deming, Harvard Graduate School of Education; Claudia Goldin, Harvard University Department of Economics; and Lawrence F. Katz, Harvard University Department of Economics. The study found that "for-profit students end up with higher unemployment and 'idleness' rates and lower earnings six years after entering programs than do comparable students from other schools." The authors also found that for-profit students "have far greater student debt burdens and default rates on their student loans."

The study notes, "Private for-profit institutions have been the fastest growing part of the U.S. higher education sector. . . . For-profit enrollment increased from 0.2 percent to 9.1 percent of total enrollment in degree-granting schools from 1970 to 2009, and for-profit institutions account for the majority of enrollments in non-degree granting postsecondary schools." The authors call this rapid expansion "phenomenal."

Nothing remotely like this explosion of enrollment took place during the same time period in the private and state sectors, where making money for owners and shareholders is not a factor. America did not see the establishment of any new Ivy League or Big Ten universities in the last few decades. If anything, not-for-profit schools have been imperiled because of the slow economy, which has hurt endowments, and the budget crises many states face.

The Harvard researchers did conclude that many honorable for-profit schools exist, and have been beneficial for many students. But the negatives were substantial. Among other findings, the researchers concluded that many for-profit schools:

- Leave students with significant debt burdens
- Increase taxpayer cost through high default rates of their students on federal loans
- Charge higher tuition and fees than public-sector alternatives
- Graduate students who "are more likely to end up unemployed" or trapped in "idleness"
- Are less accountable than non-profit schools
- Are more difficult to regulate.

In my opinion, making money should be the motivation in business, but not in education. We have to examine the practice of giving federal grants to students at for-profit institutions. If the main beneficiaries of these loans are the entrepreneurs who set up the schools, then we have to re-examine the loans to students at these schools. We can't have a situation where a few business people make a lot of money and shift the financial burden to unsophisticated student consumers and the federal government.

HEALTH CARE

The United States is the only advanced country that permits the pharmaceutical industry to charge exactly what the market will bear, whatever it wants.

MARCIA ANGELL, M.D.
(American physican and author, b. 1939)

PRESCRIPTION DRUGS

For hundreds of years, philosophers, sorcerers, and other dreamers tried to turn base metals into gold. Fabulous wealth awaited the person who managed to convert common iron, lead, or zinc into precious gold.

It was, of course, a false promise. Base metals cannot be turned into gold.

But a kind of alchemy exists today in the pharmaceutical industry, where the major companies are known as "Big Pharma." The markup on many drugs creates the sort of riches alchemists of old could only dream about. It's as though Big Pharma has turned prescription drugs into gold — for them.

Plenty of villains have been identified as contributors to the high cost of our health care system. Too many lawsuits. Too many high-paid doctors. Too much government. The lack of a single-payer system.

Everybody has their favorite whipping boy to blame for skyrocketing costs.

To my mind, one of the biggest problems in our health care system stems from the fact that the cost of prescription drugs is too high.

I had to get three prescriptions last week. They were nothing special, just drugs to help with my mild case of diabetes. The drugs I take weren't recently discovered. There is nothing exotic in the way I'm being treated. But the cost of my three prescriptions was $1,100.

Here's the alchemy part: try weighing a few of the top-selling drugs that are used to treat diabetes, high blood pressure, and cholesterol — just put the pills on a scale. At market prices, they weigh far more per ounce than gold. Unlike gold, whose price goes up and down, the cost of popular trademarked drugs keeps going up. For those of us who are covered by health insurance and are required to contribute only a small co-pay, the cost for many common drugs is hidden.

Lipitor is the blood cholesterol-reducing drug sold by Pfizer, the largest pharmaceutical company in the world. In 2011, Pfizer had worldwide revenue of $67.4 billion, net assets of almost $200 billion, and net income of $10 billion. Since Lipitor went on the market in 1996, sales have exceeded $125 billion, topping the list of best-selling branded medications for almost a decade. Pfizer also sells market leaders Viagra, Celebrex, and Zoloft, among others. The following table shows seven top-selling drugs, the cost per pill, and extrapolates that cost to show the price per ounce of the active ingredients in each. The ingredients in most pills cost little to manufacture, but they are sold for far more than the price of gold.

DRUGS	DOSAGE	PRICE PER PILL	COST PER OUNCE
Lipitor	10MG	$13	$28,313
Januvia	100MG	$9.12	$2,580
Seroquel	50MG	$8.03	$4,544
Viagra	50MG	$15	$8,490
Zyprexa	10MG	$24.26	$68,655
Concerta	18MG	$8.49	$13,363
Levitra	20MG	$15.44	$21,847

Notes:
A Prices per pill from Rite-Aid and CVS
B One ounce equals 28,349 mg.
C Most of the weight in these pills are inert ingredients.

The active ingredients in a drug such as Lipitor cost over $28,000 per ounce. The recent price of one ounce of gold in September 2013 was approximately $1,300. Why does some prescription medication cost so much more than gold?

Big Pharma would say that the cost of drugs is primarily due to the huge upfront costs of identifying potentially helpful chemical compounds, testing them in the lab and then in clinical trials, and then receiving FDA approval. This is an expensive process with no guarantee of success.

It's true that bringing a drug to market is a long,

costly, and risky proposition. But I don't think that research and development (R&D) alone accounts for the high price of drugs. If that were the case, how could these corporations afford to sell the same products for so much less outside the United States?

The respected drug-watch organization RxRights.org found that a prescription for Lipitor (10 mg, 90 tablets) cost $309.97 — $3.44 a pill — in the United States. The same prescription — same company, same dose, same ingredients — cost $80.07 for 90 tablets, or just 89 cents per pill, at an international pharmacy. The same type of wide discrepancy in pricing is found in other common medications, including Plavix and Nexium.

Drug price inflation is a problem. It's a major factor in the skyrocketing overall cost of health care in the United States.

Exactly how much are drug prices rising?

The AARP Rx Price Watch report, issued in 2010, found "retail prices for some of the most widely used brand-name prescription drugs shot up more than 8 percent in 2009, even as inflation plummeted to a record low."

The AARP did not pluck just a handful of drugs to make their case. The AARP report found that "all but six of 217 brand-name prescription drugs had retail price increases exceeding general inflation last year." Some increases were staggering: "The drug Flomax, generally prescribed for incontinence due to prostate problems had the biggest price jump, climbing 24.8 percent in 2009."

I think that the drug companies use the excessive markup in the United States to create their big profits. And those who have studied Big Pharma agree.

Perhaps the most damning study was conducted by Donald W. Light of Stanford University and Rebecca Warburton of the School of Public Administration, University of Victoria. "Demythologizing the High Costs of Pharmaceutical Research" was published in 2011 in the journal BioSocieties, which is affiliated with the London School of Economics and Political Science. The paper examines in great detail how research and development (R&D) costs are inflated, and other wide-reaching negative effects of Big Pharma policy.

The paper's final conclusion: "The mythic costs of R&D are but one part of a larger, dysfunctional system that supports a wealthy, high-tech industry, gives us mostly new medicines with few or no advantages (and serious adverse reactions that have become a leading cause of hospitalization and death), and then persuades doctors that we need these new medicines. It compromises science in the process, and consumes a growing proportion of our money."

And theirs was not a lone voice crying in the wilderness.

Merrill Goozner, senior correspondent for the *Fiscal Times* wrote, "This study strengthens the view that drugs companies do not need prices as high as they are to recover R&D costs, and their corporate risks are much lower than claimed. Most of their R&D products are scores of drugs with few proven advantages over existing drugs that can command higher, government-protected prices. Gross profits are spent more for marketing than research in order to maximize the number of patients taking these drugs. A large number of clinical trials are conducted for marketing and signing up lead clinicians."

Every year, the companies spend untold millions of dollars trying to get doctors to prescribe their drugs. "Drug companies say the millions of dollars they pay physicians for speaking and consulting justly compensates them for the laudable work of educating their colleagues," *ProPublica,* the public-interest journalism group, wrote in 2010. "But a series of lawsuits brought by former employees of those companies allege the money often was used for illegal purposes — financially rewarding doctors for prescribing their brand-name medications. In several instances, the ex-employees say, the physicians were told to push 'off-label' uses of the drugs — those not approved by the US regulators — a marketing tactic banned by federal law. In the past three years alone, pharmaceutical companies have anteed up nearly $7 billion for settlements in cases such as one filed by Angela Maher, a former drug sales rep for Ortho-McNeil Pharmaceutical."

In July 2012, the world's fourth largest drug company, GlaxoSmithKline, admitted wrongdoing in a case that clearly helps explain some of the high cost of drugs. According to an article in the *New York Times,* GSK "agreed to plead guilty to criminal charges and pay $3 billion in fines for promoting its best-selling antidepressants for unapproved uses and failing to report safety data about a top diabetes drug."

The pharmaceutical firms set a price for drugs in conjunction with the insurance companies that sell health-care coverage. They settle on a price that will be acceptable for the life of the trademarked drug, and one that, over the life of a patent, can earn a company billions of dollars in profit.

Federal law prohibits the government from regulating drug prices. So what occurs is what I call modern alchemy — sanctioned by our government.

I object to companies using the criteria of maximum profit that the customer will bear as their criteria for pricing. This keeps life-saving drugs beyond the reach of people who need them but lack the financial means or insurance to afford them.

One simple solution is to have equally powerful parties negotiate drug prices and allow the import of approved drugs. Through Medicare and Medicaid and other programs, the government is by far the biggest purchaser of prescription drugs, but is currently restricted by law from negotiating prices.

I recommend that Congress pass a new law not only allowing but also encouraging the government to negotiate with Big Pharma. This new law would save billions and put a big dent in the national debt.

OBAMACARE

Our government has long been involved in health

care in our country. Programs such as Medicare are a significant help to millions of Americans. Even free market critics of recent health law changes would be dismayed if programs like Medicare were dismantled

The Affordable Care Act (Obamacare) does represent a significant change to how health care is administered and paid for in our country. I'll give the example of how health care costs will change for my own company.

Before Obamacare, healthcare benefits cost our company $1.3 million. We pay our unmarried employees 50 percent of the cost of health care, married employees 66 percent, and executives 100 percent as part of their benefits package.

Many of the younger people don't take the insurance, even though we're paying for part of it. For a single person who works for us, insurance costs about $100 a week, so they have to contribute the other $50. These employees have an average paycheck of $400 to $500 a week. Many of them think that they are unlikely to get sick, and they don't enroll in our health care plan. We save that $50 on those employees who opt out of our insurance program.

When Obamacare fully kicks in, our companies' insurance costs will initially increase. Under the mandate, everyone will have to have health insurance. Our single employees won't be able to opt out of the plan.

But despite this, I'm strongly for Obamacare. The extra insurance will cost our company money, but it will help people currently uninsured and offer the country a far more rational health delivery system. More families will be able to receive preventative medical care, people will have a regular doctor, and there will be fewer emergency visits to hospitals. In the long run, medical costs should be cheaper.

I know we have to decrease medical costs. We have to reduce the cost of drugs, which is the biggest driver of medical costs, and we have to cut down on paperwork for insurance companies. I've heard many doctors complain that the paperwork required to process a claim today has made them unhappy with their profession. I think the biggest thing we could do to reduce costs in the system would be to adopt a single-payer system, but I'm afraid that won't happen any time soon. The European and Canadian models are amazing and I would vote for them in an instant, but given the current political climate, that kind of fundamental shift in health care delivery just will not happen.

We need to help those who can't help themselves. One of the areas the Republicans and the Democrats have fallen down on is help for the mentally ill. I have family members who have had mental problems, and I know first-hand the difficulties of helping people with psychiatric diseases. The prisons are filled with mentally ill people. Prisons cost more than health care, and the government could spend its money more wisely by helping mentally ill people rather than incarcerating them.

Some conservatives might say, "Those type of people should be able help themselves. They won't do anything to help themselves." Mental illness is a disease, not a choice. It must be a part of a complete health care solution.

POLITICS

A conservative is a man with two perfectly good legs who, however, has never learned how to walk forward.

FRANKLIN D. ROOSEVELT
(32nd US president, 1882-1945)

Politics has always interested me. In recent years, I have become more personally involved in politics and politicians. I have reached into my pocket to support progressive politicians, especially in Rhode Island, and in the process I have become one of the biggest Democratic contributors in the state.

My first political campaign was back in 1952. My parents supported Adlai Stevenson, and I helped them pass out Stevenson literature. My dad wasn't too active in politics, but he was a union member and the unions in our state supported Stevenson.

JOHN F. KENNEDY

My love of politics started with John F. Kennedy.

On November 7, 1960, the day before the presidential election, I was home on leave from the Army to attend my sister's wedding. I heard that Kennedy, then a senator from Massachusetts, would be making a last-minute campaign stop in Providence. I was already a fan of JFK, a charismatic politician with progressive ideas, and here was a chance to see him in person. I dressed in my uniform and went to the Providence City Hall, where Kennedy was to speak from the front steps. It was a mob scene when I got there. The crowd was estimated at thirty thousand, the largest in the city since President Truman had visited in 1948. Everyone loved this presidential hopeful from our neighboring state.

I wanted to shake his hand, and I figured that after his speech, he would go back inside City Hall, and leave for his motorcade via a side door. I got to that door, and was first in a growing line of people who wanted to greet him. And when he came out, I was the first to shake his hand.

What a thrill that was. I call it a "Forrest Gump" moment, a special handshake that I can still recall with warmth more than half a century later.

As far as I'm concerned, JFK was everything a President should be. Those Camelot years passed far too quickly, and Kennedy left much undone when he was killed. On the day Kennedy was assassinated, I was working on a secret government satellite project at a facility outside the Baltimore airport. Word came over the radio that the President had been shot. No one could believe it. We were all told to go home, but I decided to drive thirty miles to Washington, DC. It just seemed important for me to do.

It was late afternoon by the time I reached Washington, DC. The sadness and shock was overwhelming. JFK brought such hope to our country, and that feeling of optimism was cruelly dashed in an instant of gunfire. That afternoon, I saw a limousine driving through the streets of Washington with Bobby Kennedy in the back seat. Five years later, Bobby, who was running for the Presidency then, was shot and killed after winning the California Democratic primary.

The Kennedy family has made substantial contributions to American government. I was fortunate to meet Teddy Kennedy many times. The Massachusetts senator was a great friend of Rhode Island politicians, including Senator Claiborne Pell. Our own Kennedy, Patrick, was our local US Representative from Rhode Island. Even though I come from a totally different background, I have tried to model myself after the Kennedys when it comes to charities and politics. The Kennedys are successful people who have tried to do the right thing for all Americans.

PROGRESSIVE DEMOCRAT

The first check I ever wrote to a politician went to Rhode Island Governor Phil Noel in 1968. In 1972, I supported Joe Garrahy for Rhode Island governor and became very involved with his campaigns. Garrahy became the most popular governor of his generation and spent the last eight years of his life in my office, still helping the state of Rhode Island.

Today, I support the major Democratic candidates in Rhode Island. Everyone in my whole family is a Democrat except one of my brothers (I won't name him here).

I'm a progressive Democrat. Progressives tend to be the most liberal of the Democrats. The Republicans for a long time have been trying to make "liberal" a bad word. There's nothing wrong with being liberal. The Democrats being branded "liberals" could respond that "conservatives" are a detriment to our system because they are stuck in the same thought process and won't change their minds.

Some politics are too local and small-minded for me. I want to make a difference on a bigger scale. I meet with the state and federal candidates and give them my thoughts so they understand my positions. I contribute money to candidates to support politicians and policies I think will be good for the country.

I was perplexed that the Supreme Court ruled recently in the Citizens United case that corporations are people. But don't the judges realize that Germans, Italians, Chinese, and investors from other countries own pieces of our corporations? It's senseless to let corporations, whose ownership can be foreign, get involved in our politics.

I think we need laws to protect people from the greed of some corporations. Massachusetts Senator Elizabeth Warren is trying to write laws to protect the people. One example of the need to protect the public concerns the "paycheck" loan. Let's say you make

$400 a week. You go to the loan company and you get an advance on your $400 salary. When your paycheck comes in wo weeks later, you give it to the loan company, plus you pay a $50 loan charge. That means you're paying more than 300 percent interest on the paycheck loan. That's criminal. The government needs regulations to keep these types of companies from charging more than 18 percent per year. We need regulations to stop these sorts of crimes.

JOB CREATION

People are beginning to focus on the income gap in our country. The wealthy are getting much wealthier, while the vast majority of the population can barely keep their heads above water. The Republicans have a "trickle down" theory that the more the wealthy make, the more it helps the average Joe. But here's the fallacy of their reasoning: wealthy people don't create jobs for the middle class. They only make jobs if they can make money. Most of the time, wealthy people want to cut jobs because the fewer people they employ, the more money they make.

It's the small companies that have provided the hundreds of thousands of new jobs in the last five years. But states and municipalities continue to bid against each other to get large companies to move to their locales.

In many cases, catering to wealthy corporations can have undesirable consequences. The company moves to the new state and builds a factory. Three years later, another state courts the company, the company moves again, the factory shuts down, and the taxpayers of the state get stuck with the bill. Hundreds of towns around the country have been burned when large companies such as Walmart receive tax credits to build a store and then walk away from the store to build a larger store ten miles away in a different town because of new tax incentives.

Professional sports can be an even worse deal for a municipality. A city can build a new arena and in doing so, make a professional franchise more valuable. The owners can then sell the team for a high price. Then the new owners can move the team when they get an even better offer to move. It's a sad situation for the local municipality — higher tax bills and a team that's gone, when the municipality tried so hard to help.

WAR AND PEACE

As we exit the wars in Iraq and Afghanistan that have continued for more than ten years, the American public has made it clear that they want no more wars. They have lost faith that our government is telling the truth about why we have gone to war in the past.

It has become clear in recent years that the Bush administration misled the public on the reasons to go to war against Iraq. That war has become the biggest failure of foreign policy in our history. In ten years of fighting, these wars cost over a trillion dollars. More than five thousand American service personnel were killed, more than thirty-one thousand injured, and more than one hundred thousand Iraqi and Afghan men, women, and children have been killed. We have destroyed Iraq and did not improve Afghanistan, countries that were never a threat to us.

Our adventures in Iraq and Afghanistan of the story of "The Boy Who Cried Wolf." There has been a group of neo-cons in America who never want to miss a chance to go to war. But these recent failures of American intervention have soured the public.

> The public expects to be told honestly about threats to our country or the need to act with military force to achieve humanitarian ends. The truth always serves the best interests of our country.

Now, when a real threat comes up, the American population reacts with skepticism. The downside to this attitude is that when there is a legitimate reason to take some kind of military action, we no longer may have the will to help. In Kosovo, during the Clinton administration, our country stopped the slaughter of the Muslim minority by the Serbs and never lost a single American. It would be difficult to gain the support of the country for another justified intervention at the present time.

While I understand and even identify with most anti-war sentiment, there are sometimes events on the world stage that require an appropriate response. Our involvement in World War II worked because the whole country was committed.

The public expects to be told honestly about threats to our country or the need to act with military force to achieve humanitarian ends. The truth always serves the best interests of our country.

RACE RELATIONS

I grew up in a family environment with no racial prejudices. But in the larger world, attitudes about race are quite diverse. The cruel nature of societal prejudice became crystal clear to me after I entered the Army and was stationed in Alabama.

The Army itself had been desegregated in the 1940s. But I saw first-hand the effects of Jim Crow and segregation in the South. Alabama struck me as an alien society. I could not believe ordinary people could be so cruel to their neighbors.

Years later when I was working as a stockbroker at Kidder Peabody, I heard the news about the assassination of Martin Luther King. There were scenes of rioting on television. Our manager gathered everyone in the office and instructed us to take home our account books and important papers in case there were problems in our city. He then turned to those of us who lived in the suburban town of Barrington, Rhode

Island and said, "It's lucky for you there is only one main road into town and the police have staked it out to make sure no troublemakers come into town."

I am sure my reaction to these events, which I did not share with my manger, would have surprised him. Not only did I not take my account books home but I felt great sympathy for the black community's loss. In the projects were people of every color and background, who lived without fear of each other. That afternoon I walked up College Hill to Brown University and joined in the demonstrations against the murder of Martin Luther King, a man we now honor with a national holiday.

THE CONSEQUENCES OF LIES

Words have meaning. Words have power. This is especially the case in the television and digital age, when virtually everyone has access to the public airways and statements can be repeated over and over, whether right or wrong. The Internet has changed the game, and not always for the better.

I was very angry when Minnesota Congresswoman Michelle Bachmann abused her power with tragic consequences. During the September 2011 Republican debate, Bachmann's rival Rick Perry, governor of Texas, was under pressure for supporting the vaccine against the HPV virus, a leading cause of cervical cancer. Bachmann appeared on NBC's Today Show to criticize Perry. She said he was wrong for seeking to force "innocent little twelve-year-old girls" to have "potentially dangerous" injections.

Bachmann said, "I had a mother last night come up to me here in Tampa, Florida, after the debate. She told me that her little daughter took that vaccine injection and she suffered from mental retardation thereafter."

Bachmann had no proof that such an incident had really happened or even could. But how many parents decided not to have their daughter's vaccine based on her comments. How many girls will end up with the HPV virus, all because of a uninformed comment from a leader of the Tea Party? According to Dr. Eileen Dunne, an epidemiologist at the Centers for Disease Control and Prevention, speaking at a Congressional hearing in October 2011, there is no evidence of such an effect of the vaccine.

POLITICAL AND PHILOSOPHICAL DIFFERENCES

There are many people in this country who, because of their strict adherence to conservative dogma and political philosophy, vote against their own interests. These people often mischaracterize the motivation of people on the opposite side of the political perspective. Some of my pet peeves:

1. Many conservatives own guns and believe liberals and progressives want to take their guns away. Not so. We just need some reasonable laws so

that guns do not fall into the hands of the criminals. There have been too many mass shootings in recent years, many of which could have been prevented if reasonable gun control laws were in place.

2 Many conservatives are "pro-life" but only for the unborn, because they also believe in capital punishment. They believe liberals and progressives want to kill babies. This is obviously not the case.

3 Many conservatives think immigrants are the downfall of our country and they believe Democrats want to coddle immigrants. Our country was made great by waves of immigrants over the years, and every conservative has an immigrant in his past. We can control immigration and at the same time treat immigrants in our country fairly.

4 Many conservatives are doing well financially. They believe, often wrongly, that they succeeded by themselves, and they think liberals and progressives want to make everyone dependent on the government. Not true.

5   Many conservatives are against gay people serving in the military, teaching their children, or getting married. They also claim they are a "compassionate" political party. These two points of view don't match up.

6   Conservatives believed President Reagan when he said "government is the problem, not the solution." They have no understanding of the necessary and positive role of government in many aspects of life.

These conservatives fight against:

1   Affordable health care that does not deny coverage for pre-existing conditions.

2   A fairer tax system that would not allow the "1 percent" to dodge their fair share.

3   A safe, government-run, Social Security system.

4   A fair unemployment compensation system to protect people who lose their jobs.

5   Fair regulation of the financial

industry to prevent it from preying on the poor and middle class.

6 Environmental laws that protect us from climate change and polluters.

7 Protection of free speech and privacy laws.

HOPE FOR THE FUTURE

There are many conservatives and liberals who are sure that they are right and the other side is wrong. Although I agree most of the time with the progressives, I think we may be heading down a path that is dangerous for our country — a red state / blue state divide that bodes ill for the country.

I hope there will be a new wave of progressive politicians united under the need for a better balance between the haves and the have-nots. My life has taught me that I couldn't have succeeded without the help of my family, my friends, and my country. I hope other people will realize we all need a helping hand at some point to succeed in life.

We must recognize that we live in a world economy. Global economic forces are bigger than any one country, political system, or corporation. International companies will move their money and manufacturing to wherever they can make the biggest profit and pay the fewest taxes. Such is the nature of a free market system.

But despite what the prophets of doom maintain,

this does *not* mean we have to have to race to the bottom and pay our workers less to maintain our competitive economic position in the world. Quite the contrary. Our country has certain natural advantages that should enable us to come out on top. I believe:

1. We have the greatest educational and scientific institutions in the world. Countries from all over the world send their best and brightest here to be educated.
2. We are the breadbasket of the world and export more food than any other country.
3. We have the most robust legal system that not only protects individual rights, but also allows businesses to grow under a fair and protective government.
4. We have the most innovative products that are in demand all over the world, from technology to financials to education to oil and gas to a host of other industries.
5. We have some of the greatest natural energy resources in the world.
6. We have the biggest economy in the world, and we also have accumulated the greatest wealth.

If our future is planned correctly, we can come out on top and have all the emerging countries buying from us instead of just selling to us.

Our manufacturing base may never be the same, but our intellectual, academic, financial, and natural resources are still strong.

> Our manufacturing base may never be the same, but our intellectual, academic, financial, and natural resources are still strong.

There is a huge upside to international trade: when the economies of many countries become intertwined, there is far less likelihood of unrest among them. It is unimaginable that countries in the European economic community would start a war with each other or any of the countries in North or South America.

I look forward to a world like this in the future — mutually dependent and looking for new ways to work together.

AFTERWORD

*Success is getting what you want;
happiness is wanting what you get.*

DALE CARNEGIE
(American writer and lecturer, 1888-1955)

I turned 72 this year. I feel great, I love my work and my family, and I am excited about this book. I hope some of the lessons I have learned in my financial and personal life can help others.

But in 2011 I had a real health scare.

For a few years prior to 2011, I had a series of rather harsh morning headaches. These new headaches felt different from the migraines I had suffered with for a large portion of my life. I instinctively knew something was wrong with me.

The nagging headaches went on for approximately three years while I consulted five neurologists with little resolution. Finally, a tumor was discovered. It was growing inside the top of my skull, and pressing against my brain, producing the headaches. That was the bad news.

The good news: the tumor was diagnosed as a

benign meningioma, which is ordinarily responsive to treatment. After surgery, I recovered completely, and the morning headaches are now gone. My recovery was a difficult experience. I could not drive for six months and driving cars has always been one of my greatest pleasures! It took me many months to get my energy level back.

I have always considered myself to be self-reliant. Before the surgery, I had never fully appreciated the support that family and friends could provide. My wife was always at my bedside, questioning the doctors to make sure I was being taken care of properly. Family and friends brought me to doctors' appointments and helped in countless ways. For that, I am eternally grateful. My businesses never missed a beat, and that's a tribute to my three hundred employees, my management team and, in particular, my general managers and Nick Moceri, the president of my two largest companies.

And I learned some more lessons.

The first is obvious: our days are precious, and our family and friends are what matter in life. And good business partners and employees are a great asset, too! I learned firsthand that the saying, "you have to live for the moment" is absolutely true.

I also learned a lesson about our great nation and its people, some of who are not as fortunate as I am. I now realize the importance of quality health insurance and the advice of some of the best doctors in the country. I am frustrated for those who have none of these benefits and must go through similar experiences without insurance and family support.

We as a country can do better, and I hope that everyone faced with circumstances like mine can one day have universal health insurance and a network of supportive people around them who can help.

I'm glad to have the opportunity to share my life and ideas with others. I hope this book will encourage readers to do their part to help other people and make the world a better place. Get involved. You can make a difference!

Above all, believe in yourself. I know that my self-confidence and interest in people helped make my business career successful. Lead with your passion, and you'll have the best chance of a successful career and life.

I hope this book helps you reach your goals.

Tom DePetrillo